Of Houshold Stuff

Of Houshold Stuff:

The 1601 Inventories of Bess of Hardwick

🌳 THE NATIONAL TRUST

Front cover:
Empty arch from a set of arches containing female
personifications. Linen embroidered with gold and silver
thread and coloured silks. Height 30 cm, at Hardwick.
(NTPL/Brenda Norrish)

Back cover:
Detail of 'Patientia' (Patience) from the set of personifications.
Height 15 cm, at Hardwick. (NTPL/Brenda Norrish).
Portrait of Bess of Hardwick, attributed to Rowland Lockey,
1592. (NTPL/Hawkley Studios)

First published in Great Britain in 2001 by
The National Trust (Enterprises) Ltd,
36 Queen Anne's Gate, London SW1H 9AS
www.nationaltrust.org.uk/bookshop

©The National Trust 2001

ISBN 0-7078-0329-2

Designed and phototypeset by James Shurmer

Printed and bound in England by Biddles Ltd,
www.biddles.co.uk

Contents

Acknowledgements

This book is foremost a celebration. 2001 marks the 400th anniversary of Bess of Hardwick's extraordinary 1601 inventories, and it is highly appropriate to mark the occasion with a publication which presents all three inventories together for the first time. We are very grateful to the Furniture History Society for permission to reprint their earlier published transcript of the Hardwick inventories, and to Peter K. Thornton for allowing us to reprint his commentary accompanying that transcript. Thanks are due also to Their Graces The Duke and Duchess of Devonshire, to Peter Day, Keeper of the Collections at Chatsworth, and to Barbara D. Palmer and John M. Wasson, who kindly agreed to us including their recent transcript of the Chatsworth inventory.

No small amount of detective work has been required throughout the production of this book, and in that area we are especially grateful to Nicholas Brewster for checking the transcripts so thoroughly, and to Nicholas Cooper for providing invaluable guidance and advice on room layout at Hardwick New Hall.

Finally, we are greatly indebted to Santina M. Levey who, with uncommon grace, allowed herself to be torn away from her endeavours on the forthcoming *catalogue raisonné* of the Hardwick embroideries to work so enthusiastically on this more modest, but equally fascinating, publication.

James Parry,
The National Trust

The 1601 Inventories of Chatsworth and the Two Halls at Hardwick

by Santina M. Levey

In January 1601 inventories were taken of the Tudor house at Chatsworth and the two halls at Hardwick to accompany the will of Elizabeth, Dowager Countess of Shrewsbury. Those relating to the halls at Hardwick have been available since 1971, when they were published by the Furniture History Society with commentaries by Lindsay Boynton and Peter Thornton, but a transcript of the Chatsworth inventory has not previously been printed.

The inventory of the New Hall at Hardwick is the richest and most detailed of the three but, for a full appreciation of its contents and of the scope and value of the Countess's possessions, all three inventories are needed, although, even then, the picture is not complete. Under the terms of the Countess's will, her eldest son, Henry Cavendish, was stripped of all but the house at Chatsworth, which was his by entail. Its contents, however, were hers to bequeath, and they, together with those of the two halls at Hardwick and the halls themselves, were bestowed on her second son, William Cavendish. He was already provided with a house at Oldcotes, some three miles from Hardwick, which his mother had built and largely furnished for him, and there was also a house at Aldersgate in London which, judging from an inventory of 1617, was fitted out handsomely. These houses have to be taken into account when assessing what William inherited and what survives at Hardwick today.

The three inventories reflect the events of the Countess's life from the time of her marriage to Sir William Cavendish in 1547. The grandest house, and the one likely to have been closest to her heart, was Chatsworth. The land there had been purchased by Sir William Cavendish in 1549 and registered in both their names; together they had planned the new house, which was habitable before Cavendish's sudden death in 1557. Further work was carried out during Bess's marriage to Sir William St. Loe (1559–1565) and, in the 1570s, as the Countess of Shrewsbury, she added a third storey for the State Apartments in which she and Lord Shrewsbury entertained Lord Burghley, the Earl of Leicester and other members of the Privy Council who came to enjoy Lord Shrewbury's baths at Buxton and, no doubt, to check on Mary Queen of Scots at nearby Sheffield Lodge.

In 1584, as a result of her great quarrel with Lord Shrewsbury, the Countess moved to the Old Hall at Hardwick, taking with her many of the fine furnishings from the Chatsworth State Apartments, which she is likely to have used in the grand new rooms added to the Old Hall in the late 1580s and 1590s. As her anger with her eldest son increased and any prospect of his having a legitimate heir faded, she placed her hopes of establishing a Cavendish dynasty on her second son, William; the New Hall was to be his.

Although large and grand, the New Hall had relatively few rooms; excluding all the service rooms, they totalled only 46, compared to 55 in the Old Hall and a spectacular 97 at Chatsworth. The survival of some of the household accounts, a careful reading of the 1601 and earlier inventories, and the evidence of what remains in the New Hall suggest that it was furnished largely from the resources of the Countess's existing houses. Her only major expenditure was on wall hangings, since the New Hall was only sparingly panelled. On her last visit to London in 1591–2 she had bought four sets of tapestries, only one of which (the Story of Abraham) was new; the other three were secondhand. The most important was a thirteen-piece set of the Story of Gideon, which had belonged to Sir Christopher Hatton, as had the set 'with personages', destined for her own Withdrawing Chamber and of which no record of purchase remains. Another set, of five panels, depicted the Story of Tobit and gave its name to Tobies Chamber in the New Hall, while the remaining two sets, one of verdures and a sixteen-piece set of the Story of Nathan, were used to replace finer tapestries taken from the Old Hall in the great re-arrangement which must have taken place when the New Hall was fitted-out between 1597 and 1601.

The quantity of furnishing available in the two older houses was enormous, and the 1601 inventory of Chatsworth depicts a depleted but far from empty house; the Countess had continued to spend time there throughout the 1590s and rooms were left ready for her and other members of the family. That important visitors were also expected is shown by the fine furnishings remaining in the Nobleman's Chamber and nearby rooms. Even in those State Rooms, which had lost their textile and other furnishings, some good wooden furniture remained, like the 'fayre long table with a frame inlayde, eleven stooles, [and] three playne stooles' in the High Great Chamber.

Although no longer central to the Countess's life, the Chatsworth of the 1601 inventory still depicts a long-established and self-sufficient great house. There were workshops for a variety of craftsmen – glazier, plumber, smith, chandler – as well as a brewhouse, bakehouse and still-house. The availability of local food is suggested by the fishing nets in one of the lodges and the location of another lodge in the Cuningree or rabbit warren. The gardens were well established and provided with places for rest and entertainment, including the still-existing arbour in the vanished water garden and a number of decorative turrets, including the Stand Tower (now called the Hunting Tower) on the hill above the house.

Internally, Chatsworth was finished to a far higher standard than either hall at Hardwick. Six rooms were panelled to the ceiling, including the Matted Gallery which was 'fayre waynscotted to the height markentrie with portalls'. Twenty four others were 'waynscotted rownde aboute', including Savills Chamber, which was 'fayre waynscotted or seeled with Coulored woodes markantrie, pelasters and Carving', while 'the Parlor at the upper end of the halle' was 'fayre waynscotted with white wood & imbosted worke above the waynscott'. Some panelling was inlaid with alabaster and coloured stones, and the quality of the stone overmantels in the house is shown by one, possibly from the Muses' Chamber, which was moved to the altered State Withdrawing Chamber at Hardwick in the nineteenth century.

Chatsworth was the only house to have built-in storage units, as in 'my ladies wardrop' which was 'waynscotted with fayre presses rownde about', while the middle wardrobe also had 'fayre presses in the middest.' That wardrobe still contained spare furnishings, but the other three in the house and the presses had been more or less emptied. Left behind, however, perhaps as a sign of the changing times, were the contents of the Armoury.

Unlike Chatsworth, the Old Hall at Hardwick was full of life in 1601. Its less extensive range of workshops were busy serving both New and Old Halls, while many members of the household and some visitors continued to be accommodated in the latter. All its rooms were fully furnished and there was still a substantial quantity of textile furnishings and some furniture in the wardrobes, although that formerly used by William Cavendish was virtually empty, presumably for the benefit of Oldcotes.

The inventory suggests that the New Hall, although handsomely furnished, was not yet fully complete, notably in the service areas on the ground floor and the turrets on the roof. Only three of the turrets are mentioned and they contained miscellaneous furnishings from 'newe tickes for fetherbeds' to a large quantity of pewter-ware which, with fifteen kettles, eleven pans, three frying pans and other implements, far exceeds the equipment recorded in the kitchen and boiling house. The inventory also illustrates the consequences of the large-scale movement of the household furnishings, with misplaced items and split sets of objects like the French stools and benches, inlaid with stones and coloured woods, which appear in ones and twos in the two upper floors of the New Hall, but belong to the large sets made for Chatsworth, where most of them remain. In the wardrobe at the New Hall are parts of bed sets and spare pieces from sets of tapestries, which had hung in larger rooms at Chatsworth or the Old Hall.

The inventory of the New Hall describes the furnishings in great detail and, as Peter Thornton makes clear in his Commentary, there were relatively few pieces of fine carved or gilded wooden furniture, although these did include the Sea-dogs table, several fine inlaid tables and two or more Renaissance cupboards. But it was the textile furnishings that dominated the house, and the high esteem in which they were held by the Countess, and her expectation that they would survive for a substantial period, is made very clear by the terms of her will. The goods were not left to William for use at his own discretion; they were left in his care, and that of his descendants, in perpetuity.

'I especially will declare appoynte that noe pretended will gifte or devise to any other person or persons of the sayed former bequeathed plate Beddinge hanginges or furniture be allowed or held good in Lawe.... And I further will and especially requyer that all and euery of the sayed persons to whome the use and occupacen of the sayed plate Beddinge hanginges and other furniture so bequeathed or appoynted as aforesayed shall haue speciall care and regard to preserve the same from all manner of wett mothe and other hurte or spoyle therofe and to leave them so preserved as a foresayed to contynewe at the sayed seuerall houses as a forsayed for the better furnishyng them therewithall'.

Such expectations did not seem as strange in 1601 as they do today. Fine textiles, almost all of which were imported, were costly status symbols which held their value, and many of the furnishings recorded in the inventories were already old. For example, the black velvet bed embroidered with metal thread, purl and pearls in the Pearl Bed Chamber of the New Hall dated from the time of the Countess's marriage to William Cavendish in 1547, while several other beds can be identified in a 1553 inventory of Chatsworth and had probably been transferred from Sir William's former country house of Northaw in Hertfordshire, which he had sold in 1551. Several sets of tapestries are likely to have followed the same route, probably including the fifteenth-century hunting tapestries, now in the Victoria and Albert Museum, which may be the set of large 'hanginges with personages and forrest worke', which in 1601 was divided between the hall and the Countess's bed-chamber in the New Hall. Certainly many of the finest textiles installed in the State Rooms on the top floor of the New Hall had been made during the 1570s for the State Apartments at Chatsworth.

The only furnishings for which the Countess acknowledged the inevitability of decay were those made of linen; with the exception of two beds with new hangings of embroidered linen in the New Hall and eight pairs of sheets and a little table linen at Chatsworth, the three houses are without sheets and pillow cases, table and washing linen or any type of cloth for use in the kitchens or for cleaning. Sixteenth-century laundry methods were pretty brutal and the turn-over in domestic linen was rapid. Only at the end of the New Hall inventory was any linen listed – many unused lengths of plain, diaper and damask linen and some exceptionally fine items decorated with embroidery and lace; it represented a substantial capital investment, as did the gold and silver plate with which it is listed.

None of the plate and only one identifiable piece of linen has survived, but the New Hall nonetheless still contains many of its original furnishings. These include a substantial number of its original portraits, the rare painting of *The Return of Ulysses* and the *verre eglomisé* panel or 'glass with my Lady's arms'. Also uncommon are the magnificent fire dogs or 'payre of brass Andyrons' in the High Great Chamber, the two brass chandeliers, now in the Gallery but originally in the Entrance Hall, and the lone survivor of the 'great glass Lanthornes' from the staircase landings. More than half a dozen pieces of sixteenth-century furniture remain, together with the largest collection of tapestries, embroidery and other stitched textiles to have survived in the care of a single family for over four hundred years.

These survivals were due to a fortuitous set of circumstances. Firstly, Henry Cavendish, unable to pay for the refurnishing of the Chatsworth State Apartments, sold the house to his brother William, so the two houses remained in the care of the same branch of the family. William's descendants decided to develop Chatsworth as their main country seat, and although Hardwick was not left untouched, its State Rooms escaped the constant upgrading that took place at Chatsworth. Once the false association of Hardwick with Mary Queen of Scots had taken root in the eighteenth century, the older furnishings in the State Rooms were more consciously treasured, even if the danger from excessive attention was sometimes as damaging as neglect.

It is not surprising, however, to find that, of the ninety-eight surviving pieces of embroidery and needlework and the six whole or part sets of tapestries which can be identified in the 1601 inventory of the New Hall, all were in the State Rooms, except for the tapestries in the Countess's Withdrawing Chamber, on the floor below. Interestingly, some of the tapestries now at Hardwick were not there in 1601, but can be identified in the 1553 and *circa* 1562 inventories of Chatsworth. Similarly, two distinctive needlework table carpets, dated 1574 and 1579 and which do not feature in any of the inventories, must have been at Oldcotes or, less likely, in London in 1601.

The existence of the inventories adds enormously to our understanding of the surviving objects and, conversely, the objects bring vividly to life the written descriptions in the inventories.

A Short Commentary on the Hardwick Inventory of 1601

by Peter K. Thornton

I wrote the commentary below in 1970–71, thirty years ago. I have made no alterations to the text itself, but the glossary has been slightly adjusted by Santina Levey. I am pleased that this little essay has been retained for this new publication. It was a very early exercise in setting down such material in a rather novel way, not just dealing with furnishings as individual antiques, but also trying to deduce how furnishings were used and functioned as an ensemble. As Keeper of Furniture at that time at the Victoria and Albert Museum, it fell to me to write this short piece. It pointed the way to my *Seventeenth Century Interior Decoration* (Yale University Press, 1978), which went out of print only recently. I shall probably now write a sequel.

Note:
The term 'copper', used in two places in the commentary (p. 14, 3rd para, and p. 18, 2nd para), does in fact mean 'brass'. It is curious that the second reference in the inventory itself comes immediately before the entry 'foure plate candlesticks *of brass* to hang on the wales', as if brass were different from copper. The inventory clerk must have been misled by the shiny reflectors of the wall sconces, as contrasting with the cast brass of the chandelier 'with severall places to set lightes in'[N.H.50]. Their surfaces do, of course, look different.

P.K.T, 2001

We can deduce quite a lot about the habits of the occupants of Hardwick Hall from a careful reading of this inventory. For example, we can tell that the Countess of Shrewsbury suffered from the cold, for she took elaborate steps to exclude it from her Bed-Chamber and the adjacent With-drawing Room.[1] Among her defences against the rigours of the Derbyshire climate were two window-curtains of warm red cloth, which were supplemented by 'three Coverletes to hang before a windowe' (presumably one of the two windows in her room was more draughty than the other), while there was another coverlet 'to hang before a dore' and 'a counterpoynt of tapestrie [to hang] before an other dore'. Her bed was also hung with 'scarlet', which implies that the material was of fine woollen cloth and not of silk, like the hangings on most of the other grand beds in the house. These warm hangings were richly trimmed with silver and gold lace and with gold fringe, so they must have been rather striking, although they were definitely not as sumptuous as those on some of the other beds and it is clear that Lady Shrewsbury had been prepared to sacrifice splendour for comfort when choosing this material.[2] The bed was also provided with five curtains of purple 'bays'. Particularly expensive bed-hangings were sometimes furnished with protective covers or special dust-curtains, but such measures would hardly have been necessary for the red and silver set just mentioned, and one can only conclude that this additional set of curtains was required for warmth.

On the bed, the Countess had two quilts covered with linen (so they were clearly not for show) and three pairs of fustian blankets,[3] as well as six Spanish blankets.[4] In order that she should not have to stand on the cold floor when she climbed out of this exceptionally snug bed, she had no less than eight warm mats on the floor around the bed.[5] In her With-drawing Room she had window-curtains of darnix,[6] which was also a warm material, while part of the room could be divided off by a 'travice [traverse] like a skreyne covered with violet Coulored Cloth layde about with black lace'. There was also a screen covered with green cloth in the room. Both rooms were, moreover, hung with tapestry – one set having figures and Lady Shrewsbury's arms on them, the other being a set of verdure tapestries ('forest work'). The mistress of this recently-built house was, of course, an old lady when the inventory was made in 1601, so it is not surprising that she should have felt the cold. Hardwick, with its huge expanses of glazed window, must have been a particularly cold house.[7]

'My Ladies With-drawing Chamber' seems to have been more in the nature of a large private closet into which she could withdraw from the more public life which was led in the other principal rooms of the house; it served a purpose different from that of the modern drawing room which is essentially a reception room even if it may also have served as a 'sitting room'. A glance at the inventory will show that it was richly appointed but must have been cluttered with furniture in an almost Victorian manner; clearly no effort was being made to produce a unified scheme of interior decoration – of the kind which was to become fashionable in England after the Restoration – where all the furnishings for a room were designed en suite. The same remarks apply to Lady Shrewsbury's Bed-Chamber.

It is to be noted that she had 'a foote turkie Carpet' (a Turkish 'foot carpet') in the With-drawing Room. This is a relatively early instance of a carpet being used on the floor. Many of the carpets mentioned in this and other inventories of the period were in fact covers of various degrees of richness and elaboration that lay on tables and the like. In the same room, for instance, there was 'an inlayde borde [table ?]' and 'two grene cloth Carpetes for it'.[8] The other Turkey carpet in the room may in fact also have lain on the floor, since it is not listed in association with a table; but it is not designated 'a foot-carpet' as would have been usual at this time. In the Bed-Chamber there were 'too foote Carpetes of turkie worke' which, of course, implies that they were pile-surfaced rugs woven in England in a technique similar to that used by the Turkish rug-weavers in Anatolia.

The Countess had many chests and coffers in these two rooms. She probably kept valuables in them; her clothes are more likely to have been housed in the trunks that stood in the adjacent passage-way and in the Maid's Chamber next door. The small coffers and the box bearing her coat-of-arms and that of her husband, on the other hand may well have been for documents. These items are listed immediately after 'three deskes covered with lether' and the 'lyttle deske to write on guilded'. These desks will certainly have been of the portable type, with a sloping surface on which one could write. One placed them on a table and some had hinged tops giving access to a space with compartments within, like a modern school desk – but without legs. Since no standish (with ink-horn and pounce-pot) is mentioned, it is likely that at least one of the desks contained these essential articles. At any rate, it is clear that Lady Shrewsbury carried on her extensive correspondence from this Bed-Chamber; she had no separate Study. She kept only six books in her room which included a work by Calvin. In the Bed-Chamber there also stood the bed of the Lady Arabella Stuart,[9] so the room must have been rather crowded. In the With-drawing Room were 'two Chares for children', which indicates that the younger members of the family also spent much time in these rooms.

It is possible that her Ladyship had a watch among her jewellery (which is not listed in this inventory) but there were no clocks in her rooms. However, she did have an hour-glass. There was a pair of bellows in the fireplace in the Bed-Chamber; these were something of a rarity at the time. The fireplace contained two pairs of andirons – copper ones for decoration and a pair of practical ones of iron.[10] The previous item in the list was a wicker screen which must have been a fire-screen. In fact, this was the commonest sort of fire-screen at the time.[11] It was probably circular with a wooden stand. Several screens of this type are in the house; they are mostly modern but one seems to be of a certain age.

There was a 'little roome within My Ladies Chamber' (i.e. it could only be reached by going within, or through, the Bed-Chamber) and this housed her close-stool which would have been a box-like seat with a hinged lid. It may have had a leather seat although this is not stated. It was covered with blue cloth with white stitching, and had three pewter basins so that a fresh one was always in place while the others were being emptied. The Lady Arabella's own close-stool stood alongside it. Modern writers often lead one to believe that our ancestors were totally lacking in delicacy and always had their close-stools standing in their bed-chambers, but this was by no means always the case. There are many indications that this necessary piece of furniture usually stood in an adjacent closet or at least in a cubby-hole in the wall, discreetly hidden by a door set into the panelling. The King of France may perhaps have received his subjects enthroned on his close-stool but most other people seem to have preferred to relieve themselves in private. Of course, some rooms were furnished with chamber-pots but it is probable that these were mostly brought in at night-time.

Considerable trouble was taken to counter unpleasant smells at this period. In many inventories, one sees mention of 'perfuming pans' which must have been vessels in which one burned scented pastilles. A favourite way of scenting the air and one's linen was by means of 'sweet bags' which contained sweet-smelling herbs. These bags were often most richly embroidered and were regarded as highly acceptable presents.[12] Among the long list of linen at the end of the Hardwick inventory, mention is made of 'a sweet bagg of Chaungeable taffetie' (i.e. of shot silk) which seems to have been a relatively humble example. Lady Shrewsbury must in fact have owned many far more elaborate specimens. They were probably listed among her wearing apparel; at any rate, they are not mentioned in this inventory.

The Countess had a bed of scarlet cloth, as we have already noted. The bed-curtains were 'stript downe' with silver lace. This presumably means that the silver was applied in vertical stripes, probably along the seams joining the widths of red material. This bed only had three curtains, one to each of the exposed sides (the head being against the wall and furnished with a 'bedeshead') and these must have been fastened together by means of the 'red silk buttons and lowpes' after the Countess had retired. It was more usual to pin the curtains together and perhaps the five purple 'bays' curtains were closed in this manner.

Most of the beds at Hardwick had curtains that were less elaborately decorated than the valances – the pelmet-like borders depending from the tester. The Countess's bed was no exception; the valances were embellished with embroidered motifs executed in gold thread with borders of gold and silver lace, and with gold fringe along the bottom. The bed-posts were also sheathed in red cloth with silver trimmings.

The Lady Arabella's little bed had 'a Canapie' of blue and white darnix. The fact that the bed is described as having a canopy and not a tester implies that it had only two curtains which hung from a crown-like canopy suspended above the head of the bed. This was not an uncommon form of bed in the sixteenth century and may be regarded as the ancestor of the half-tester. However, this canopy had three curtains and I can only suggest that the third formed a sort of head-cloth.

There were several beds in the house which seem to have been considerably more magnificent than the two already mentioned. That in the 'Pearle Bed-Chamber' had a carved and gilt bedstead and double valances (the curtains ran between each pair of valances, there being an inner and an outer valance on each of the three sides of the bed). The hangings were of black velvet embroidered with gold and silver thread and studded with pearls. The valances were additionally trimmed with a black, gold and silver fringe. There were five curtains to this grand bed; presumably one at the foot-end and a pair on each side. The counterpane was also exceedingly richly worked with pearls and coiled silvered wire ('purle').

Even more striking seems to have been the bed in the 'best bed-Chamber' which had 'a fayre lardge sparver' instead of the more usual tester. A sparver was a form of tester suspended from the ceiling by cords.[13] It could have valances like the rigid type of tester that was supported by bed-posts, and both types had a head-cloth or 'bedeshead'. This bed was presumably an ancient one, for beds with sparvers had probably not been made for some decades. However, the bed was exceptionally rich, as the description proves, and people were still not so ridden by fashion in those days as to worry overmuch whether their old furniture was in keeping with the latest mode or not. They may have followed the dictates of fashion in their clothes, and any new furniture they acquired would have been modern in style, but they were in no hurry to discard the furniture of their grandfathers, as long as it was sufficiently splendid. Their grandchildren, on the other hand, had no such scruples and tended to throw it all out in order to make room for entire suites of new furniture in the latest Continental style. This is presumably why so little Elizabethan furniture survives at the house. There is a certain amount from the 1630s or so, and more from the 1690s; but the Elizabethan must largely have been discarded once it was old.

This fine bed had six curtains, which was the maximum possible (i.e. two per side). They ran between double valances. The counterpane was of 'Cloth of tyssue[14] payned with cloth of gold'. The word 'paned' indicates that, in this instance, the central panel (or pane) was of cloth of gold and that the borders were of cloth of tissue. The term is often rendered as 'impaned'.

There were other grand beds in the house but none were as splendid as those in the 'pearl' and the 'Best' bed-chambers. That in the 'turret Chamber' is interesting because it had 'Pantes to go about the sides of the bed at the bottom'. In French, the word 'pentes' was given to the four panels, fitted to rich table-carpets, that fell down the sides of the table; the same term must sometimes have been used to denote the lower valances of a bed, as here, although the usual French name for these was 'soubassements'.

'Within the Best Bed Chamber' was a little room in which stood an elaborate field-bed with rich hangings.[15] It presumably could be taken apart and carried off on campaigns, if necessary. It had a quilt of some exotic material (Chinese or Indian) described as 'India stuff imbrodered with beastes'. One bed-chamber contained a carved and gilt bedstead which seems to have been in the form of a ship. This and the bed in 'Tobie's Chamber' (so known on account of the tapestries which depicted the story of Tobias) both had five curtains, the latter set being trimmed with 'parchment lace of golde and silke' which was 'layde ... over the seames'. The valances were trimmed with, amongst other things, 'bone lace' which derives its name from the bobbins, usually of bone, used in its creation on the lace-makers' pillow – from which it derives its other name of 'pillowlace'.

The word 'chamber' normally implied that the room contained a bed at this period, but one exception to this was the 'High Great Chamber' which was obviously a reception room as was the adjacent Gallery. Here stood rows of stools (including three French ones inset with pieces of marble) and chairs, all richly upholstered, as the list shows. In the Gallery were no less than nineteen 'long quitions whereof one for the Chare' [just mentioned in the inventory and probably a very grand affair], the rest for the windowes'. These long cushions are described at great length and must have constituted eye-catching features of the room. They are decorated in various ways with elaborate embroidery and must have been the pride of Lady Shrewsbury who was, of course, an exceptionally accomplished needlewoman. Some of the cushions described in the inventory are still to be seen at Hardwick.[16] Although these particular cushions mostly lay on the window-seats, it was not an uncommon practice to place them across the arms of armchairs, as many contemporary portraits show.

The Gallery contained two striking looking-glasses which were rare objects at that period.[17] The walls were hung with tapestry but there were also numerous portraits. It is by no means impossible that the latter were hung in front of the tapestries as were the heavily framed paintings shown in many of the engravings of Abraham Bosse dating from the 1630s. Tapestry hangings were still treated with very little ceremony at this date! There were also some paintings and tapestries on the walls of the High Great Chamber, where there was a looking-glass painted with the Royal Arms of England, presumably on the glass.

On the first floor lay the 'Lowe Great Chamber'. This seems to have served as a dining hall and contained the usual long table, two square tables[18] and a cupboard which was provided with two table-covers or 'carpets', suggesting that it had two tiers or shelves and was perhaps what elsewhere would have been called a court-cupboard. Although described as 'turkie Carpetes', one had Lady Shrewsbury's arms inwoven, and this rather suggests that they were really of turkeywork and were not from the Near East – although sixteenth-century Turkish carpets specially woven with a European owner's arms are not unknown. There were several upholstered forms which must have been used at the long table. The richly upholstered chairs would have been for the head of the household and her family. It may have been on account of the Countess's susceptibility to cold that the windows were furnished with curtains of 'grene penistone' – presumably a woollen material woven at the place of that name which lies not far from Hardwick. However, she probably only dined there on special occasions, for she had provided herself, when she built the new house in the 1590s, with a 'dyning Chamber' – then quite a recent innovation.[19] It is described as being 'little', and contained a draw-table, a chair covered with turkeywork (probably quite an impressive piece of furniture intended for the Countess), a stool covered with the same material (for the Lady Arabella?), and fourteen uncomfortable 'Joyned stooles' which had no cushions and must have been for the favoured members of the household who were allowed to join her in this little room.

Provision was also made for a larger number of people to dine in the Hall on the ground floor. It contained three long tables with six accompanying forms, but there was no other seat-furniture. The room was probably used by the humbler members of the staff. There was a screen at one end of the Hall which supports a bridge connecting, at first floor level, the Low Great Chamber and Lady Shrewsbury's Withdrawing Room. From this small gallery one would have had a good view of the hall below and the 'too great Copper Candlestickes with several places to set lightes in'. These large chandeliers were suspended with ropes from the ceiling of the Hall, which, of course, reached up through two floors. There were also some 'plate Candlestickes of brass to hang on the wales'. These must have been sconces with brass, plate-like reflectors of the kind one sometimes sees in sixteenth-century illustrations. There are some in the house which may possibly be of the period.

This is not the place to discuss the equipment of the kitchen, or the contents of the cellar; nor need we dwell on the long list of plate. The list of household linen is of interest but is mostly self-explanatory. It is only necessary to know that the most expensive form of linen material was linen damask. 'Diaper' was less costly since it was only figured with squares or lozenges in the weave. Cambrick and Holland were plain but came in several qualities.

The enormous quantities of linen required in such a household may well surprise a modern reader, but then the richness of Hardwick Hall at this period is also astonishing, especially when one recalls how remote was this house, perched on its hill in Derbyshire. As the furniture historian runs his eye down the list of contents, however, he cannot but be struck by the fact that the total effect in a great house of the period was achieved largely with the aid of sumptuous textile furnishings and hardly by means of wooden furniture at all! An unusually high proportion of the Elizabethan textile furnishings of Hardwick has survived and serves to give some idea of the splendour of such a late sixteenth-century house. Even so, what we now see is a faded image of its original glory.

1 Plans of the house are reproduced on pp. 66–67. It is difficult to be certain about the location of some of the lesser rooms. However, the position of the principal rooms can be established.

2 Woollen cloth came in an exceedingly wide range of qualities at that time and the finest ranked with the less costly ranges of silken materials. Fine scarlet cloth was one of the most expensive. Although much of the present commentary is concerned with textile furnishings, for reasons which should become apparent, this is not the place to discuss technical questions connected with antique textiles. Nor is it the place to consider the exact identity of the various classes of textile mentioned in the inventory. We await with great interest the publication of Mr. John Nevinson's studies of the textiles at Hardwick, and hope that Mrs Florence Montgomery and Miss Natalie Rothstein will one day find time to publish the glossaries of ancient textile terms that they have been compiling for so long. In the meantime an excellent survey of the whole field is given by George Wingfield Digby in his *Elizabethan Embroidery*, London, 1963.

3 The name fustian seems to have been applied to various materials and much uncertainty still surrounds its identity. It was usually made of cotton, but some fustian woven at Norwich in the late sixteenth century was of worsted yarn. It is possible that it was a mixture of cotton and worsted.

4 Woollen blankets from Catalonia, often known by the name 'Castelognes' in French.

5 The mats were, in fact, 'fledges', made of a thick, coarse wool called fledge.

6 Darnix or dornix derived its name from the city of Tournai (Doornick), which was famous for its tapestries and for its upholstery materials of wool and linen. Darnix was probably decorated with comparatively large patterns, because it was used for window-curtains, bed-hangings, and similar objects of some size. It is also likely to have been a wide material. The '*haute-lisseurs*' of Tournai (who were not, in this case, weavers of tapestry) are known to have woven wide furnishing-materials of wool and linen. Examples of materials of this general class may be seen in most big collections of ancient textiles and it seems likely that at least some of them must be the elusive 'darnix'. According to a list of customs duties, published in 1582, one class of darnix had some silk in it (T. S. Willan,

A Tudor Book of Rates, 1962). Darnix must, at any rate, have been easily identifiable at the time.

7 'Hardwick Hall, More glass than Wall', as the local rhyme has it.

8 Since these carpets were merely of cloth (i.e. a plain woollen material), they were probably just protective covers for the delicate inlay on the table-top. 'Borde' could mean table; in this instance it may mean a games-board. Other tables at Hardwick were described as such. They mostly had 'carpets'.

9 She also had her own bedroom next door but it only contained a bed and some wall-hangings.

10 Andirons were, of course, used in association with a wood fire. In one room at Hardwick, however, there was an 'iron for sea-cole' – in other words, a grate.

11 In the 1601 inventory of the old house at Hardwick, mention is made of a 'twiggen skreyne' which must somehow have differed from the more common wicker ones. Perhaps it was coarser.

12 Digby (op. cit., pp. 69–72) describes many fine 'sweet-bags' but suggests they may also have been to hold comfits (sweet-meats). The fact that there was a sweet-bag among the linen at Hardwick, however, would seem to indicate that they were more like the modern sachet.

13 When suspended at the four corners, such a tester came to resemble a hovering sparrow-hawk, (Fr., *épervier*).

14 It seems that this was a silken material displaying much metal thread.

15 There was another field-bed in the 'Prodigall Chamber'.

16 See Digby, op. cit., pp. 110–12, for a description of nine such cushions still at Hardwick.

17 Lady Shrewsbury had no mirror in her Bed-Chamber although there was one decorated with her arms in her With-drawing Room. It is still there.

18 One of the square tables was inlaid with pieces of marble, and also with black and white wood—a reminder that much of the wooden inlay of this period originally produced a striking effect. The intended strong contrast between the light and the dark wood has mostly long since been lost by fading and obliterated by dirt.

19 The term 'Dining Room' was occasionally used, but the more common name for this room was 'Dining Parlour' – especially when it was essentially a hived off section of the old Eating Hall.

The Inventories

The Transcripts

Three copies were made of the Countess's will and the inventories of her three houses; two are in the Public Record Office (Prob. II/111/ff.188–92 & Prob. 10/254) and the third is in the archive at Chatsworth. It is the Chatsworth copy which is transcribed here. It consists of eight and a half sheets of vellum, each 22½ inches (26.6 cm) deep by 32 inches (57.3 cm) wide, of which two contain her will and one and a half the Chatsworth inventory. The remaining five sheets are devoted to the inventories of the two halls at Hardwick; one and a half for the Old and three and a half for the New Hall. All the sheets are signed and sealed by the Countess.

The transcripts of the two Hardwick inventories are the work of the late Lindsay Boynton, who expanded all abbreviations, altered *i* and *y* to conform with modern usage, and added some punctuation. The first sheet of the Chatsworth inventory has been transcribed by Barbara D. Palmer and John M. Wasson, and the half sheet by Nicholas Brewster. In these transcripts all abbreviations have been expanded, but the spelling and punctuation remain as in the original.

The Houses

Of the three houses, only the New Hall at Hardwick remains substantially as it was in 1601; the Tudor Chatsworth was converted through a series of major alterations into an eighteenth-century mansion with extensive nineteenth-century additions, while Hardwick Old Hall is now a semi-demolished ruin. Mark Girouard has produced a convincing plan for the Tudor Chatsworth, suggesting the location of most of the major rooms mentioned in the 1601 inventory (Girouard, *Country Life*, 1973), and English Heritage has published a ground plan of what remains of the Old Hall (Worsley, 1998), but only for the New Hall are there detailed plans which make possible a more direct correlation with the rooms described in the inventory. Consequently it is only these plans that are reproduced here.

The Inventorie of the ffurniture of houshold stuff which is ment and appoynted by this my laste will and Testament to be remayne and Contynewe at my house at Chatesworth according to the true entent and meaning thereof

In the high gatehouse Chamber, a mattriss, a pallet Case, an inlayde Chare & the same Chamber verie fayre waynscotted with Coulored woodes set out with portalls and some alablaster and other stone. In the Inner Chamber, a playne bedsted a fetherbed a mattriss a bolster a pillowe, three fledges a Coverlet, a playne forme, too joyned stooles, too quitions a payre of bellowes. In the next Chamber, a playne bedsted, a mattriss a quilt three Coverletes, a joyned stoole, a Landyron for seacole, a fyer shovell. In the Armorie black Corsletes for back and brest twelve. fyftie and nyne payre of splentes for bill men, fortie sixe peeces of mayle, seven sulletes, eight sculls, a Jack, three flask boxes, twentie peeces of harnes and Iron at the least, twentie and eight black bills, twoo bowes, seaven arrowes, a partizan a holberd fyve bills, a saddle for a great horse, a bearrell to Dress mayle, three tops of stills & too bottoms, a brass pott, a fane for the top of a house, too mouldes of lead a bedsted a Cubberd with tills, a playne forme, a Dripping pan, too little Iron bounde Cofers, a mark of lead to mark sheep, and the said armorie waynscotted. In the middle gatehouse Chamber seven peeces of olde tapestrie hanginges, a feild bedsted, a tester and Curtins of blewe cloth fringed and laced, a fetherbed a bolster too pillowes too mattrisses a pallet case a grene Coverlet of buckerom quilted, foure fledges too flannells, too Carpetes of blewe cloth laced, a long quition of velvet and Cloth of golde too tapestrie quitions a little square borde, a lyverie Cubberd, a joyned stoole, three Close stooles whereof one Covered with Cloth. In the Inner Chamber to the middle gatehouse Chamber, a playne bedsted, a tester of Damask blewe & yellowe, a mattriss too fledges a Coverlet of tapestrie, a little inlayed stoole. In the little Chamber at the lowe leades dore a bedsted a fetherbed, a mattriss, too blanketes a Coverlet, a bolster, a lyverie Cubberd, a playne borde to brush on In Batemans Chamber, a bedsted, a tester and Double vallans of Capha, a fetherbed a mattriss a bolster foure blanketes, a Covering of tapestrie a lyverie Cubberd to the sayde Chamber waynscotted. In the Inner Chamber to Batemans Chamber a mattriss a fetherbed a bolster a Coverlet, a little paynted borde. In Mr Talbotes Chamber a bedsted paynted grene, a tester and vallans of grene Damask with pictures, Curtins of saye, a mattriss a fetherbed a bolster three fledges a Court Cubberd an inlayde Chare a Joyned stoole, the same Chamber waynscotted with portalls In the Inner Chamber to mr Henry Cavendishes Chamber a a bedsted a mattriss a fetherbed a bolster too fledges a Coverlet, the same Chamber waynscotted. In mr Henry Cavendishes Chamber a bedsted a matriss a fetherbed a bolster three fledges a quilt of Carnation taffatie a quition of turkie worke, a Chare inlayde, a joyned stoole, a Cubberd, a borde to brush on at the dore, the same Chamber waynscotted. In the little Closet at the wardrop Dore, the head and feete of a bedsted, a stone morter. In the storehouse, three boxes, too great Chestes bounde with Iron, some peeces of bedstedes, three little pewter bottles, too glasses a Case of glass, nyne barrs of Iron, a grate of Iron, three grates of lead, too Curtin rodes, a payre of tables, a bowe, too quivers, a payre of bellows. In my Ladies wardrop, seven yardes of Canvas, a black velvet footestoole, a borde to brush on, three joyned stooles, the same wardrop waynscotted with fayre presses rownde about. In the little Closet within the high wardrop a servantes bedsted, a tester, a buckler. In the vtter wardrop a bedsted a Coverlett. In the little Closet at the wardrop dore a bedsted an alablaster Candlestick. In a little vawte there, a frame to weyve Carpetes, a Dripping pan. In the middle wardrop too fledges foure coulered fledges, foure peeces of tapestrie hanginges seaven Coverletes sixtene blanketes, too quilted Counterpoyntes of sarcenet, a Canapie of ashcoulored saye printed, a Canapie of velvet Damask and valure black, a bedes head of Damask and taffatie, some peeces of taffatie Curtins, a tester and vallans of fustean & Canvas, a Canapie of rowde sacking, a Canapie of black velvet imbrodered, a Canapie of Crimson sattin and grene tinsill with grene saye Curtins, a tapestrie quition lyned with lether, an Irish quition too Carpetes of blewe clothe a flanell, too peeces of Canvas of seventene yardes, an other peece of seven yardes, some peeces of blewe hanginges, a little Chare of black valure, a fetherbed tick, a bolster tick, too long table clothes of Diaper, too diaper towells, a square Cubberd cloth of diaper foure saye Curtins too yellowe too grene, three sarcenet Curtins, too Irons for a sparver, eight wood Cofers whereof one with tills, too Iron bounde Cofers, a payre of virginalls, a short tent, twenty and three pewter dishes, a great pewter plate a pewter bason eight pewter plates seven Chamber potes, a warming pan foure brass waytes, a sumpter a little joyned stoole, a frame for a Canapie a grene Deske, a folded Chare the same wardrop waynscotted with fayre presses in the middest. In ffynishers Chamber a bedsted paynted grene, a tester and Curtins of grene cloth stitcht and frenged, a Carpet of purple cloth garded with velvet & fringed a square borde an inlayde Chare an inlayde stoole, too playne stooles, a quition of tapestrie, the same Chamber fayre waynscotted markentrie. In worme Chamber six peeces of red Cloth hanginges a field bedsted a tester and Curtins of grene cloth with black lace a fetherbed a mattriss three fledges

11. Inner chamber to 12

12. Mr Henry Cavendish's Chamber

13. Little closet at Wardrobe Door

14. Storehouse

15. My Lady's Wardrobe

16. Little closet in High Wardrobe; 17. Outer Wardrobe

18. Little closet at Wardrobe Door; 19. Little Vault

20. Middle Wardrobe

21. Finishers Chamber

22. Worm Chamber

a Rigg, a bolster a pillowe, a Carpet of black cloth garded with velvet, an other Carpet of black cloth, two Cubberdes, an inlayde Chare, a stoole Covered with nedleworke, a little stoole Covered with Churchwork too playne stooles. In the Inner Chamber to worme Chamber a bedsted a pallet Case, a mattriss a bolster too fledges a blanket, too Close stooles a Chamber pott. In the Erle of Leycesters Chamber a blanket too formes a joyned stoole. In the withdrawing Chamber to the Erle of Leicesters Chamber, a stoole, a peece of Canvas of seven yardes a Coverlet a fier shovell. a Closet to the muses Chamber fayre waynscotted to the height and shelfed. An Inner Chamber to muses Chamber waynscotted french panell. In the high great Chamber a fayre long table with a frame inlayde, eleven stooles inlayde, three playne stooles, three Coverletes on the harthes, the same Chamber all verie fayre waynscotted with Coulored woodes markentrie and set fourth with planetes In a Closet there a bedsted, and waynscotted. In the high gallerie, an inlayde table, a flanell to Cover it fourtene inlayde stooles an inlayde forme, three olde Coverletes, six paynted candlestickes an instrument with virginalls, the same gallerie verie fayre waynscotted with coulored woodes markentrie & pelasters fayre set foorth In Savills Chamber, a square borde inlayde, a Carpet of tawnie cloth garded with velvet, a stoole imbrodered, a Canapie of Crimson sattin with golde lace and sarcenet Curtins, a peece of white fustean, three sarcenet Curtins, a Coverlet on the harth, the same Chamber all verie fayre waynscotted or seeled with Coulored woodes markantrie, pelasters and Carving. In the Rownde turret, a vane for a house guilded, the same turret verie fayre waynscotted & with alablaster black stone and other devices of Carving. In the gatehouse turretes a bedsted a forme, a Clock. In a Corner turret, a Joyned stoole, an Iron ladle for a plumier the same turret and three other Corner turretes waynscotted. In an other turret a bedsted and fayre waynscotted with Coulored woodes & piramides. In the withdrawing Chamber to the Scotes Quenes Chamber, a borde Covered with grene cloth, a Coverlet. A Closet there waynscotted. In the Inner Chamber there a bedsted, a Canapie of velvet and cloth of golde with sarcenet Curtins. In the Servantes Chamber a bedsted a quilt of sarcenet a Coverlet a pallet case, a Close stoole, the same Chamber waynscotted. In the matted gallerie a Cubberd a square table inlayde, a Chare Covered with cloth of golde, a Chare Covered with black velvett, a Chare Covered with grene velvet, eight lowe stooles Covered with velvet and other stuff, a forme Covered with Damask, the same gallerie fayre waynscotted to the height markentrie with portalls. In the lowe great Chamber a long table a grene Carpet on yt, seventene joyned stooles a square borde, a grene Carpet on it fringed, a Cubberd, a lether Chare, an inlayde Chare, a payre of Iron Andyrons a foote Carpet, a quition of tapestrie, too blewe cloth formes too other formes Covered with Cloth garded with velvet, a payre of virginalls, fyve peeces of grene cloth hanginges garded with blewe and stitch with white. A Closet at the end of the great Chamber waynscotted. In tymes Chamber, fyve peeces of tapestrie hanginges of the storie of Saloman, an inlayde table a fledg to Cover it, a Cubberd, foure Darnix Carpetes, one turkie Carpet, a tawnie velvet quition imbrodered with golde a grene cloth Carpet for a long borde too Joyned stooles, a forme covered with purple cloth and garded with velvet In noblemans Chamber, ffowre peeces of Cloth of golde and velvet hanginges, a Carpet of the same stuff to the Cubberd there, a bedsted, a tester and vallans of yellowe white and grene velvet, Curtins of white and grene Damask, a mattriss a fetherbed a quilt too bolsters too pillowes, a fledg a long quition of nedleworke, a quition of Cloth of golde and tawnie velvet, a Chare covered with cloth of Tyssue and with golde and silver frenge, a little Chare covered with stript sattin, a lowe stoole covered with cloth, too turkie Carpetes a square borde a Cubberd, too Joyned stooles too Curtins of Darnix for the windowes. In the Closet there a Cubberd, a Carpet of tawnie cloth garded with velvet, a little inlayde stoole, a skreyne, a Curtin of Darnix for the windowe, the same closet waynscotted and shelfed. In the Inner Chamber a bedsted paynted with grene and golde, a tester and vallans of blewe sattin & golde spotes, a quilt of the same stuff, a Coverlet too fledges a bolster a fetherbed a mattriss a wood Chare a Court Cubberd, a Close stoole covered with fiugred sattin, a turkie Carpet, a Curtin of grene saye for the windowe, the same Closet waynscotted In the Servantes chamber a bedsted paynted with sondrie Coulers and golde, a tester imbrodered with armes a mattriss a bolster a Coverlet, the same Chamber waynscotted. In the blewe gallerie eleven peeces of blewe cloth hanginges stitch with white, a Court Cubberd a square borde too Carpetes of blewe cloth stitch with white a forme Covered with blewe Cloth, a turkie quition. In the vpper Chapple Eight peeces of blewe cloth hanginges garded with white, one hanging of black cloth, a forme Covered with blewe cloth and grene silk frenge a Chare of tawnie and yellowe velvet a long quition of Capha a turkie Carpet a silk Curtin, a quition of tapestry a joyned stoole. In a Closet above the lowe great Chamber a bedsted. In the Chapple Chamber, fyve peeces of tapestry hanginges, a bedsted a tester and vallans of red Cloth a grene sarcenet quilt, a red rugg, too blanketes, a fustean, a flanell, a fetherbed a mattriss too bolsters too pillowes, an inlayde Chare a tapestrie quition, too stooles Covered with velvet, a tawnie velvet quition too joyned stooles a square borde, a Cubberd, too Carpetes of blewe cloth garded with white and yellowe veluet, a grene saye Curtin in the windowe, a fier shovell In the Servantes Chamber, a bedsted a tester and vallans

45. Closet at end of Great Chamber; 46. Tyme's Chamber

47. Nobleman's Chamber

48. Closet

49. Inner chamber

50. Servants Chamber

51. Blue Gallery

52. Upper Chapel

53. Closet above 44

54. Chapel Chamber

55. Servants Chamber

of Damask, a mattriss a fetherbed, a bolster, a pillowe too fledges, a Coverlet, a Court Cubberd, a Close stoole covered with red cloth, a quition of tapestrie, a stoole pan too Chamber potes, a Joyned stoole, the same Chamber waynscotted. In the lowe gatehowse Chamber seven peeces of red cloth hanginges, a bedsted, a tester of Crimson sattin, Curtins of mockadowe, a mattriss a fetherbed too bolsters too pillowes a payre of flanells too fledges a quilt of lynnen cloth, a stoole covered with velvet and cloth of golde a long nedlework quition, a quition of tapestrie an inlayde Chare, a Joyned stoole, too Cubberdes too Carpetes of blewe cloth garded with white a Close stoole. In the Inner Chamber there, a bedsted, a mattriss a Coverlet of tapestrie a little Cubberd a Close stoole, a stoole pan a Chamber pot, the same Chamber waynscotted to the height. In the Inner Chamber to Ellins Chamber, a bedsted, a tester of sattin bridges a mattriss a fetherbed too bolsters three blanketes, a Cubberd, too inlayde stooles, a little quition of Churchwork too great Cradles, too little fetherbedes for them, a bolster a saye Curtin, the same Chamber waynscotted. In Hellens Chamber fyve peeces of grene cloth hanginges, one red cloth hanging, twoo Darnix hanginges in the windowes a feild bedsted, tester and Curteyns of grene cloth layde with black lace and frenged with grene and black, a mattriss too fetherbedes, a bolster, a pillowe foure fledges a Coverlet an inlayde Chare twoo Cubberdes too Carpetes of grene cloth, too joyned stooles a long quition of Crimson sattin, a payre of flannells, a little inlayde stoole, a Close stoole, a stoole pan a Chamber pot, an Iron bound Cofer, too Landyrons, In the grene gallery seven peeces of grene cloth hanginges a pallet case a mattriss a fetherbed a bolster three blanketes a Coverlet, a great Cubberd. In purple Chamber, three peeces of Darnix, a bedsted, a tester of scarlet with Double vallans imbrodered with golde, too mattrisses, too blanketes a Covering of tapestrie a bolster, a Chare, a stoole Covered with blewe cloth stitcht with white, a quition of tapestrie, too Cubberdes a grene cloth Carpet, too little inlayde stooles, a playne stoole. In the Inner Chamber to purple chamber a bedsted a mattriss a fetherbed a bolster a pillowe three blanketes too fledges, a little inlayde stoole, a stoole Covered with Damask and cloth of golde a playne stoole, a Cubberd a stoole pan a Chamber pott. In the Closet to the maydes Chamber too great Chestes, a Desk with tills, a Colander of earth, a glyster pipe with a Case, the same Closet waynscotted. In the maydes Chamber, a bedsted, a tester and vallans of Capha, a mattriss a fetherbed a bolster, three Fledges a Coverlet an alablaster morter, a Chamber pott, too stoole pans, the same Chamber waynscotted to the height and presses to laye stuff in. In the Lobby or roome over the skreyne a long table paynted, three formes an inlayde Chare a trunck a skreyne too fyer shovells, a mattriss a fetherbed a bolster too blanketes a Coverlet, a peece of grene cloth to brush on, the same rome waynscotted. In my Ladies withdrawing Chamber, too square bordes, a Court Cubberd inlayde, an inlayde Chare, a Chare Covered with cloth of golde, a foote Carpet a grene Carpet, a little stoole Covered with russet velvet, a stoole Covered with blewe cloth and stitch with white, fowre Joyned stooles, a fier shovell, too grene saye Curtins in the windowes, a great Iron bounde Cofer a peece of Darnix to Cover it, a little inlayde stoole, a payre of Iron landyrons, the same Chamber verie fayre waynscotted Deep french panell markantrie. In my Ladies bed Chamber, a bedsted, a tester vallans and postes Covered all of black wrought velvett with golde lace and golde frenge, Curtins of black Damask all trymmed with golde lace, a mattris a fetherbed, three bolsters too quiltes four fledges, three flannells a pillowe, three fusteans about the bed foure fledges about the bed, a Chare covered with Crimson velvet, a little stoole of Churchworke, too turkie Carpetes, a little borde to Drawe out, a Court Cubberd, too red cloth Curtins in the windowes, a looking glass, a frame to set it on, an Iron for a Chymney, a payre of tonges a skreyne. An other feild bedsted, tester vallans and Curtins of grene cloth trymmed with white, a mattriss a Downe bed a quilt too bolsters three fledges, an other mattriss, a fetherbed a bolster, three fledges a tawnie velvet quition, a Joyned stoole, the same Chamber verie fayre waynscotted to the height with Coulored woodes. In the Parlor at the vpper end of the halle, a Cubberd an inlayde stoole, the same parlor fayre waynscotted with white wood & imbosted worke above the waynscott. In mrs Knyvetons Chamber a bedsted, a tester and Double vallans of Damask fringed and braunched with golde, a mattriss a fetherbed too bolsters three blanketes too fledges a Chare covered with grene cloth, a Court Cubberd a Curtin of grene saye, a table. In the Inner Chamber, too bedstedes a fyer shovell a Chamber pott. In Crumps Chamber a bedsted a mattriss a fetherbed a bolster, too fledges a Coverlett a table, a Chare Covered with black velvett a stoole Covered with nedleworke. In mr Owens Chamber a bedsted a mattriss a fetherbed too bolsters three fledges, a Coverlet of tapestrie a Cubberd. In the Halle, too long tables seaven formes a Cubberd a great Landyron, the halle waynscotted. In the Chamber next to the Dyning parlor a bedsted a tester and Double vallans of Capha a mattriss a fetherbed too fledges a bolster a blanket a Coverlet of tapestrie, an other bedsted, a mattriss a fetherbed, a bolster two fledges a Chare, the same Chamber waynscotted. In an other Chamber by the lowe gallerie a bedsted too mattrisses too bolsters foure blanketes too Coverletes. In an other Chamber there too bedstedes too mattrisses three Coverletes too bolsters three blanketes a quilt. In an other Chamber there, a bedsted too mattresses too bolsters three blanketes three Coverletes. In an other

66. My Lady's Withdrawing Chamber

67. My Lady's Bed-chamber

68. Parlour at upper end of 73

69. Mrs Kniveton's Chamber

70. Inner chamber

71. Crump's Chamber

72. Mr Owen's Chamber

73. Hall

74. Chamber next to Dining Parlour

75. Chamber by Low Gallery

76–79. Three further chambers and one room by Low Gallery

Chamber there, too bedstedes a mattriss a fetherbed a bolster, too fledges too Coverletes too Cubberdes too stooles a table. In an other roome there an hundreth and fyve and thirtie lumps of Iron, three great wimbles an olde brass pott. In the lowe Chapple, a Cubberd a pulpit fyve formes, some part of the Chapple waynscotted. In a Chamber within the Chapple a bedsted a mattriss a fetherbed a bolster three fledges a Coverlet a little table a forme. In the Chamber within the Lodge, a bedsted, a tester of Capha a mattriss too fetherbedes too bolsters a fledg, a Coverlet a blanket a pillowe a wood Chare. In the Lodg a bedsted a fyer shovell, too long fyshe netes and a bowe net, a long table a forme. In the gatehouse three formes. In the Lowe wardrop a Cubberd, too long tables, a great alablaster morter, too quiltes, too red velvet quitions, a quition of tapestrie, three peeces of olde quitions, a pallet Case of sacking, too brass potes three spites, a Landyron, too black Jackes, nyne stoole panes, twentie and three Chamber potes, fyve plate Candlestickes, a Copper bason, three score and one little Iron dishes, foure dozen and too pewter dishes, fowrtene pewter plates three sawsers a posset pot of pewter, a payre of ballans and some smale waytes, thirtene brass Candlestickes, twelve pewter Candlestickes, a Chafer and Copper bason, a brass Chafingdishe too perfuming pans, a great Iron fyer shovell, eleven payre of tonges, three less fyer shovells, too Landyrons a payre of gardners sheeres, a Lymbeck a trunck an Iron bound Cofer a tankerd, too wood Chestes, a watering pott, a black bill, a great olde bible, a Colander, a pewter pott. In the little Chamber next the lowe wardrop, a bedsted a mattriss a fetherbed a bolster too fledges a Coverlet a blanket a valure quition a stoole, too wood cofers, a little borde. In the next Chamber there, a bedsted, a tester of Capha, a mattriss a bolster a fledg, a coverlet three wood Chares a borde a Close stole a stoole pan. In the north lowe gallerie, a mattriss too pillowes a great wood Chest, a brode board a stoole. In a Chamber on the side of the north lowe gallerie, too bedstedes too mattrisses a fetherbed, too bolsters three blanketes a fledg too Coverletes. In an other Chamber there a bedsted three mattrisses a fetherbed three bolsters fyve blanketes foure Coverletes a Close stoole a bill. In an other Chamber there, a bedsted too mattrisses fowre fledges a blanket three Coverletes a bolster a Chare covered with grene cloth too stooles. In the Dayrie, a long board, foure brass pans a brass pott, too payre of tonges, a fyer shovell, a great brass morter, eleven boles, six earthen potes, too Churnes a brandyron, a great bathing tubb, a hogshed, a payre of slinges a bedsted a Chamber pott too firkins fowre kittes. In the kytchin six brass pans six brass potes, three payre of rackes, eight spites, three payre of pothookes, three Dripping pans, a frying pan, a Chopping knife, foure bordes, a forme, a pestle and morter of brass, a Colander, an Iron pott, fortie pewter dishes, twelve sawsers a beif forke, three tubbs. In the Pastrie, a long borde a hogshed. In the Larder too Joyned stooles a square borde a long borde, a great wood Chest, three pewter dishes a great barrell a little firkin a bedsted a kymnell a brass pott. In the great kytchin, fyve long bordes, three fleshhookes a Landyron a brandreth. In the Pantrie too Cubberdes too binges too formes three stooles, a broken Cubberd a bason and Ewre of earth a square borde fyve brass Candlestickes too pewter Candlestickes, a great Iron bound Cofer a bedsted a mattriss a fetherbed a bolster too fledges a Coverlet, too Cubberd clothes a towell, a Diaper napkin. Plate in the Pantrie, a bason and Ewre white, a salt with a Cover white too guilt boles too white boles whereof one hath a Cover too Candlestickes. In the buttrie a Cubberd a stoole. In the Sellor eight hogshedes. In the upper Chamber in the turret over the Dungeon too bedstedes a mattriss a fetherbed, a bolster a pillowe too fledges a Coverlet a folded stoole a forme too bordes. In the middle Chamber in that turret a bedsted a mattriss a fetherbed a bolster a pillowe three fledges, a Coverlet too stooles a borde. In the lowe Chamber a bedsted a fetherbed a bolster a pillowe a Coverlett a Cubberd a borde a Chamberpott. In the upper Chamber over the gatehouse a pallet Case, a rownde table. In the middle chamber too bedstedes a mattriss a bolster a fetherbed too blanketes a Coverlet a borde too stooles a Cubberd an inlayde Chare. In the lowe gatehouse, three bedstedes a mattriss a quilt a blanket too Coverletes a borde a forme. In the lowe Chamber in the north turret a bedsted a fetherbed a pillowe a mattriss a bolster too blanketes foure fledges too Coverletes a Cubberd, a Chare Covered with valure, a quition of valure, a stoole, a borde, a fier shovell, a Candlestick, a Chamber pott. In the upper Chamber there, a bedsted an olde tester and Curtins of saye, a Close stoole. In the Glasiers roome, a bedsted fyve Casementes a vice of lead, too bordes. In a Chamber over the Colehouse, too bedstedes. In the washhouse a bedsted, too great brass potes, a great brandyron, fyve tubs, a Cofer too bordes. In the Smythie a long table a stythie of Iron. In the Backhouse too bedstedes a mattriss a fetherbed a bolster too blanketes a Coverlett too kneading troughes, a boulting bynge a Chest to put bran in fyve long tables a bread bynge a Cofer, a payre of bellowes a brandyron a brass pan a kytt. In the Brewehouse three fattes a Cooler a Lead, sixtene hogshedes eight tubs a tun Dishe a worte trough a great brass pan foure Copper kettills too skopes. In the Plumerie a bedsted a pan to melt lead, an olde broken Iron pott. In the Chaundlers Chamber a brandyron a trough to make lightes, a long borde. In the Kyln house a lead waight of a hundreth waight, a heare. In the Corner Chambers, fowre tubs a bedsted a stoole, twoo strikes too shovells. In the stable a bedsted too mattrisses. A Turret at the bridg end fayre waynscotted. In a Turret in the mount, an alablaster table a Coverlet on it, the same turret fayre waynscotted. In the stillhouse a bedsted foure stills, too pewter potes a little Cubberd bordes to set glasses on too payre of tonges. In the Chamber over the stillhouse, a bedsted a Chest too bordes. In the South garden turret too bedstedes a mattriss too bolsters too blanketes a Chamber pott too Coverletes. In an other turret a bedsted. In the arbor an alabaster table. In the Stand, a bedsted a mattriss a fetherbed too blanketes a Coverlet a bolster a table. In the Lodg in the Cuningree, a mattriss too blanketes a Coverlet. In several places in the said howse eight payre of sheetes.

Notes (by room number)

7   The Low Leads Door gave access to the flat, leaded roof at a lower level than the turret tops. As at Hardwick, the roof was a place for recreation from which the surrounding views could be enjoyed.

8   Bateman was possibly a former gentleman servant, although he is not given the title 'Mr'.

10   Gilbert Talbot, who married Mary Cavendish (Bess's youngest daughter), was the second son of the 6th Earl of Shrewsbury and succeeded him as 7th Earl.

12   Henry Cavendish was the eldest son of Sir William Cavendish and Bess. Chatsworth was entailed on him but, by a 1603 codicil to her will, its contents were bestowed on her second son, William Cavendish.

21   Given its position next to the Wardrobe, this room was probably allocated to the furnishers or upholsterers who worked in the house.

22   The surviving pair of red satin cushion covers decorated with strawberry plants and little gold worms [N.H.20] may have been part of the *en suite* furnishings for this room. Alternatively, the Cavendish snake or worm may have been a dominant feature.

24   Both Bess and the Earl of Shrewsbury were friends of the Earl of Leicester, who stayed at Chatsworth during the 1570s.

25–27   The adjacent chambers and closets to the Muses Chamber are described, but not the room itself. It may have been an alternative name for the Earl of Leicester's chamber and the fine overmantel of the Muses, now in the Withdrawing Chamber at the New Hall, may have come from there.

31   Sir George Saville, who may earlier have been a gentleman servant at Chatsworth, married Mary Talbot, daughter of Lord Shrewsbury. The couple stayed at Chatsworth in the 1570s.

39   Mary Queen of Scots was in the charge of the Earl of Shrewsbury from 1569 to 1585; she lived mainly at Sheffield Lodge and at other of his houses but, with Queen Elizabeth's permission, was occasionally allowed to stay at Chatsworth.

42   This, and other 'servantes chambers' throughout the three houses, could have accommodated a single servant or, as the presence of pallets attests, two or more. The lack of punctuation in the original document usually means the position is unclear (but see 64).

43   Chatsworth, which was finished to a higher standard than the two halls at Hardwick, may have had good wooden floors. The Matted Gallery, however, was covered with joined strips of plaited rush matting, as was the Gallery in the New Hall, where the floors were of an ash-based cement.

46 The name is likely to be a reference to Tyme or Timothie Pusey who, having joined the household in the late 1580s or early 1590s, became Bess's trusted steward at Hardwick and also her legal adviser.

47 This room was presumably reserved for the Privy Councillors and other noblemen who visited Chatsworth during the 1570s.

58/59 Helen or Ellen Steward was the housekeeper at Chatsworth.

64 Despite the final 's', there was only one bed in this room, which would have belonged to Bess's personal maid.

69 Jane Knyveton or Kniveton (née Leche) was Bess's younger half-sister and lifelong companion. She also had rooms at the Old and New Halls [O.H.39, N.H.48].

71 James Crump or Cromp had been Bess's Steward for very many years from the time of her marriage to Sir William Cavendish. He oversaw the building of Chatsworth.

72 Owen was one of Bess's gentleman grooms, to whom Lord Shrewsbury took great exception during their quarrel. He refused to say why.

74 The Dining Parlour was the 'Parlor at the upper end of the Halle' [68], where members of the family ate in private. The Little Dining Chamber served the same purpose in the New Hall [N.H.28].

100–102 These three rooms were one above the other in the same turret.

103–105 These three rooms were similarly arranged in the Gatehouse.

126 The hill rising behind the house is called the Stand, and the Tudor turret or tower, which was built as a place from which to watch a hunt, is now known as The Hunting Tower.

The Inventorie of the Plate and other Furniture of howshold stuff which is ment and appoynted by this my laste will and testament to be, remayne and Contynewe at my house or howses at Hardwick according to the true entent and meaning thereof

In the olde building at Hardwick

In the wardrop: a tester for a feild bed of wrought cloth of silver stript in panes with golde and silver lace, a whole vallans to it of wrought cloth of silver with golde and silk frenge rownde about, Fyve Curtins to it of Tinsill stript red and purple and lyned with Callico, a Counterpoynt of China cloth of golde with a pane of white imbrodered with yellowe and grene silk lace and frenge, and lyned with blewe taffaty, a Tester and bedes head of red cloth layde on with twyst of white thred and fringed with white and red silk frenge, with double vallans and fyve Curtins of red cloth sutable to it. An other Tester bedes head and vallans of red cloth stript with golde lace in panes, the vallans fringed with silk and silver frenge, fyve Curtins of red mockadowe to it. An other tester bedes head and vallans for a feild bed of Carall frenged with Cruell frenge, the vallans Indented with three little guilded knobs, Fyve Curtins of Carall sutable to it. An other tester bedes head and vallans for a feild bed of white damask and yelloe sattin, the vallans Cut with hartes, fowre Curtins of grene and red saye, three Curtins of yellowe and russet taffatie, a Curtin of taffatie Sarcenet, a Curtin of grene taffatie, a long turkie Carpet, too square turkie Carpetes, a Carpet of grene Cloth, a long peece of hear coulored brode cloth to Cover the stuff, a lardge Canvas over the stuff, an other lardge Canvas under the stuff, too other peeces of Canvas for a press, a peece of lynnen Cloth to lyne a hanging, a Counterpoynt of tapestrie, a long quition of murry and tawnie velvet, an other long quition of cloth of gold and cloth of silver paned with golde lace with black silke and golde frenge lyned with yellow and black sattin bridges, an olde quition of Cloth of golde lyned with murry velvet, a long quition of stript black taffatie and cloth of golde fretted with golde lace and lyned with blewe sattin bridges, a quition of black stript taffatie and a pane of Cloth of golde, lyned with black sattin bridges, a quition of black stript velvet and too panes of Cloth of golde lyned with murrie sattin bridges, a long quition of russet velvet lyned with black damask & with watchet silk frenge, a long quition of white tuftaffetie and cloth of golde lyned with black sattin bridges, an olde black velvet quition garded, a long quition of Cloth of silver imbrodered with golde and Crimson velvet lyned with yellowe sattin bridges, a long

1. Wardrobe

quition paned with black velvet and white tuftaffetie imbrodered with flowers of sattin lyned with black sattin bridges, a long quition of red damask stript with silver lyned with Carall, a little quition of Cloth of golde tyssued lyned with purple velvet, a long quition of yellowe taffetie, a long quition of black wrought velvet set with silver studes with silver frenge and lyned with black tuftaffetie, A long quition of black velvet fretted with white velvet with black silk and silver frenge, lyned with black damask, a Chare of Cloth of golde with purple silk frenge and foure guilt knobs. A Lytter lyned with purple velvet fringed with golde and purple silk frenge with a lace of golde and purple silk and too leaning quitions of watchet sattin fastened to it, too Coverletes and a blanket to Cover it. A Sestern of Copper with too ringes, fyve Iron bounde Chestes, twentie and three rownd boles of brass, a brass Candlestick, twentie and three brass Cockes, too brass Chafing dishes, an Ewre of brass, a payre of brass skales, a brass pott, a brass posnet, a waight of brass with the Quenes armes on it, a lead waight of half a hundreth waight, a Sallet Covered with velvet and golde lace. In the utter roome to the Wardrop: Too bedstedes, fyftene fetherbedes, fyftene bolsters, three pillowes, a mattriss, a diaper quilt, Eight Coverletes, too Counterpoyntes of tapestrie, fyve blankets, a peece of darnix, a little Clock, a sumpter of lether, a great Iron bounde Chest, too wood Chares, too Close stoles, a stoole pan, a Canvas to cover the bedding, too Lanthornes, a Jack of male quilted, a broken bell. In the lowe wardrop: a playne table uppon tressells, three fetherbed tickes, three bolsters, three peeces of old grene cloth hangings, twelve Covers for stooles of turkie worke, Fyftie and one peeces of guilt lether wrought, thirtie and foure peeces of guilt lether silvered but not fynished, a great flat Iron bounde Chest, a fier Shovell, a holberd, a bill. In the Chamber at the lowe wardrop dore: a bedsted with turned postes, a bolster, a blanket, a peece of red and grene saye, a stoole covered with grene cloth, a Joyned stoole. In the Chamber at the Forrest great Chamber dore: a feild bedsted with head & turned postes, a tester bedes head and vallans of Cloth of golde and cloth of silver stript with goldsmythes worke, the vallans fringed with yellowe and red silk frenge, fyve Curtins of blewe taffatie, a mattriss, a fetherbed, a bolster, too pillowes, too blanketes, a Counterpoynt of tapestrie, a Chare of clothe of golde fringed with golde and black silk, a table, a Carpet of darnix, a Joyned stoole, a Close stoole, a stoole pan, a Chamberpot. In a pallet there: a mattriss, a fetherbed, a bolster, a blanket, a Coverlet, waynscot rownde about the same Chamber to the top. In the Forest great Chamber: sixe peeces of lether hanginges guilded and paynted seaven foote and a half deep, a long table the frame and postes being Carved, a Carpet of grene cloth for it, a lyverie Cubberd inlayde, a Chare of Cloth of golde with golde and silk freeze, a stoole of

Cloth of golde and grene and black velvet, a joyned stoole inlayde, an Iron to set in the Chymney, waynscott under the windowes. In a Chamber at the side of the Forrest greate Chamber: a bedsted with postes, a tester bedes head and vallans of white damask imbrodered with braunches, the vallans fringed with white red and grene silk frenge, a mattriss, too fetherbedes, a bolster, a pillowe, too blanketes, a tapestrie Counterpoynt, a Close stoole, a stoole pan, a Chamber pott, a bill. In the bed Chamber to Forrest great Chamber: Fyve peeces of tapestrie hanginges with personages nyne foote deep, a bedsted with head and postes Carved and inlayde, a tester bedeshead and double vallans of Cloth of golde and purple sattin with golde and purple silk frenge, and the bedes head with armes in it, a Counterpoynt of purple taffetie imbrodered rownde about with letters and armes in the myddest and frenged with golde frenge, Fyve Curtins of purple and yellowe taffatie, a mattriss, a downe bed, a diaper quilt, a bolster, too pillowes, a payre of fusteans, a spanishe blanket, a Rugg, a table, a turkie Carpet for it, a Cubberd, a turkie Carpet for it, a Chare of Cloth of golde fringed with golde and purple silk frenge, a stoole of cloth of golde with golde frenge, a Joyned stoole inlayde, a long quition of purple sattin imbrodered and letters on it lyned with blewe velvett, a peece of darnix, a fustean and too peeces of lynnen about the bed. In the withdrawing Chamber: a playne table, a grene Carpet for it, a twiggen skreyne, waynscot round about the same Chamber to the top. In the bed Chamber the best lodging: six peeces of tapestrie hanginges with personages nyne foote deep, a bedsted with head and postes guilt and inlayde, a tester of murry and tawnie velvet imbrodered with double vallans fringed with golde and murry silk, the tester and bedes head having armes imbrodered in them, Fyve Curtins of red and yellowe silk damask trymmed with golde and red silk lace, a Counterpoynt of Cloth of golde and purple sattin stript, a mattriss, a downe bed, a diaper quilt, a bolster, too pillowes, a payre of fusteans, a spanishe blanket, a Rugg, a square table, a turkie Carpet for it, a Lyverie Cubberd, a turkie Carpet for it, a Chare of Crimson velvet garded with imbrodered worke of golde with Crimson silk frenge, a stoole of fugred sattin with a golde and silk frenge, a stoole of tawny velvet with too letters and fringed with golde & silk frenge, an Inlayde stoole, a Joyned stoole, a longe quition of Crimson velvet garded with imbrodered worke of golde with tassells and frenge of Crimson silk, a skreyne of grene buckerom, too brass Andyrons, a fustean, a peece of lynnen and a peece of buckerom about the bed, waynscott under the windowes. In a Pallet there a Canapie of yelloe and white buckerom printed, with black, white and yellowe frenge, a mattriss, a fetherbed, a bolster, a quilt of Crimson taffatie, a Rugg. In the withdrawing Chamber: nyne peeces of tapestrie hanginges varders vj of them xj foote deep, ii of

7. Chamber at side of 6

8. Bed-chamber to 6

9. Withdrawing Chamber

10. Best Bed-chamber

11. Withdrawing Chamber to 10

them ix foote deep, and one iiij foote & a half deep, a lyverie Cubberd with turned postes Carved, a turkie Carpet for it, too Chares carved and guilt covered with black stript taffaty, too long quitions of purple velvet layde on with brode golde and silver lace with silver frenge and lyned with watchet sattin bridges, too stooles inlayde, waynscott under the windowes. In the Inner Chamber to the best lodging: a bedsted, a mattriss, a fetherbed, a bolster, a pillowe, a yellowe blanket, a Counterpoynt of tapestrie lyned, a long quition imbrodered, a Close stoole, a stoole pan, waynscott rounde about that Chamber to the top. In the Gallerie by the best lodging: a forme covered with black wrought velvet, garded with grene velvet, a forme of yellowe and red silk damask garded with grene velvet, a stoole of cloth of golde tyssued & black wrought velvet with yellowe and blewe silk frenge, waynscot rownde about that gallery to the top. In the Hill great Chamber: a long table with postes and frame Carved, a grene Cloth Carpet for it, too Cubberds, too turkie Carpets for them, too formes, waynscott rownde about that Chamber. In the Corner Chamber over Mr. William Cavendishe's Chamber: fyve peeces of tapestrie hanginges of forrest work iiij of them xj foote and a half deep, the vth but ix foote deep, a darnix hanging at the bedes head, a feild bedsted with bedes head inlayde and postes Carved, a tester for it of red cloth imbrodered with white twyste, single vallans of red cloth sutable with white & red silk freng, a bedes head and fyve Curtins of red cloth sutable, a mattriss, a downe bed, a linnen quilt, a bolster, too pillowes, a Rugg, a blanket, a Counterpoynt of tapestrie, a folding table, a Carpet of grene cloth to it, a lyverie Cubberd, a Carpet of grene cloth to it, a Chare of crimson velvet & stript taffatie with red silk frenge, a stoole of cloth of golde, a joyned stoole, a Close stoole pan, a Chamber pott, a fier shovell, a payre of tonges, waynscott under the windowes. In a pallet there a mattriss, a fether bed, a bolster, a blanket, a Coverlet. In the Corner Chamber next the Court: Fyve peeces of tapestrie hanginges of forrest work iij of them xj foote and a half deep and ij of them but nyne foot deep, a bedsted with turned postes fluted, tester and vallans of red saye imbrodered with flowers and fringed with red, grene and white Cruell, Fowre Curtins of white and red saye fringed with white & red Cruell, a mattriss, a fetherbed, a bolster, too pillowes, too blanketes, a tapestrie Counterpoynt, a table, a Carpet of Scarlett garded with blewe velvet with silk frenge, a Chare, a forme, a square quition of nedlework, a fier shovell, a payre of tonges, a Close stoole, a stoole pan, a Chamber pott, waynscot under the windowes. In the pallet there a mattriss, a fetherbed, a bolster, a blanket, a Coverlet. In the Inner Chamber to that Chamber: too bedstedes whereof one with head & turned postes, a tester of purple velvet imbrodered, single vallans of purple velvet imbrodered Fringed with yellowe and white silk frenge, too mattrisses, too fetherbedes, three bolsters, fyve blankets, too Coverletes, a Chamber pott. In the Inner Chamber to the Corner Chamber over Mr. Cavendishes Chamber: a bedsted with fluted postes, a tester and bedes head of blewe cloth, single vallans of blewe cloth, layde on with white bone lace fringed with white and blewe silk, fyve Curtins of blewe Cloth sutable, a mattriss, too fetherbedes, a bolster, too pillowes, too blanketes, a Counterpoynt of tapestrie, a folding table, a Carpet of darnix, an olde Chare with a back of russet wrought velvet, a Chamber pott, waynscott rownde about the Chamber to the top. In Mr. Digbies Chamber: a bedsted, a borde on tressels, a Landyron, waynscot under the windowe. In Mr. Reasons Chamber: a bedsted seeled with tester of wood and turned postes, a mattriss, a fetherbed, too bolsters, too blanketes, too Coverletes, a square table, a Carpet of grene cloth, a Chare, a Joyned stoole. In Mr. Manners his Chamber: Fyve peeces of tapestrie hanginges with personages, nyne foote deep, a bedsted with head and postes turned, a tester and bedeshead of blewe cloth sticht with white and single vallans with white and blewe silk frenge, fyve Curtins of blewe cloth sticht with white, a Counterpoynt of red and yelloe Capha, a mattriss, a fetherbed, a diaper quilt, a bolster, too pillowes, a payre of fusteans, too blanketes. In a pallet there a mattriss, a fetherbed, a bolster, a blanket, a Counterpoynt of tapestry lyned, a table, a Carpet of blewe cloth, a Cubberd, a Carpet of grene cloth, a Chare of red cloth fretted with grene & stitcht with white & grene silk frenge, a lowe stoole of grene cloth fretted with red & stitcht & fringed with white, a plane joyned stoole, a payre of brass Andyrons, a twiggen skreyne, a peece of darnix, a Curtin for the windowe of red and grene saye, a fyer shovell, a payre of tonges, waynscot under the windowe. In the Inner Chamber to Mr. Manners Chamber: a bedsted with head and postes Carved and guilt, a tester of purple velvet imbrodered with flowers, single vallans rownde about imbrodered with flowers & with silk fringe, a pallet case, a fetherbed, too bolsters, a blanket, a Coverlett, a Counterpoynt of tapestrie, a Cubberd, a forme, a Close stoole, a stoole pan, a Chamber pot, waynscot rownde about to the top. In Mr. Fortescues Chamber: Fyve peeces of tapestrie hanginges, varders nyne foote deep, a bedsted with head Carved and guilt & postes turned and guilded, a tester and bedes head with armes of cloth of silver and taffetie script with golde, double vallans of the same stuff with gold and silk frenge and garded with imbrodered worke of golde twist, fyve Curtins of blewe damask, a quilt of purple taffetie, a mattriss, a downe bed, a Cloth quilt, a bolster, too pillowes, a payre of fusteans, a blanket. In the pallet there, a mattriss, a fetherbed, a bolster, a blanket, a Coverlet, a peece of darnix and too peeces of lynnen about the be[d], a borde, a turkie Carpet, a Cubberd

18. Inner chamber to 15

19. Mr Digby's Chamber
20. Mr Reason's Chamber

21. Mr Manner's Chamber

22. Inner chamber to 21

23. Mr Fortescue's chamber

inlayde and Carved, a stoole of cloth of silver with silk and silver fringe, a lowe stoole of Crimson fugred sattin, a twiggen skreyne, a Close stoole, a stoole pan, waynscott under the windowes. In the Inner Chamber: a bedsted, a mattriss, a fether bed, a bolster, a pillowe, too blanketes, a Counterpoynt of tapestrie, a lyverie Cubberd, a joyned stoole. In my Ladies Chamber: seaven peeces of lether hanginges paynted and guilded, a bedsted with postes Covered with purple velvet imbrodered with purple twyste and lace, vallans and bedeshead of Crimson sattin imbrodered with divers Coulered silkes & frenged with red & yellowe silk frenge, a tester of red and yellowe tuftaffetie, three Curtins of blewe and white damask paned and layde on with black silk and silver lace, an other playne bedsted, fyve peeces of darnix, a Cubberd, waynscott under the windowes. In the Inner Chamber: eight peeces of darnix, a Cubberd, too footestooles of wood, a payre of Iron andyrons, a payre of bellowes. In the sceeled Chamber next my Ladies with drawing Chamber: a square borde, waynscot rownde about to the top. In my Ladies withdrawing Chamber: too Curtins of darnix, a table, a turkie Carpet for it, a little table, a Cubberd inlayde, a Carpet for it of russet cloth, a forme, a wicker skreyne, An Iron for seacole, waynscot rownde about the Chamber to the top and a Chare of lether printed. In the long gallerie: nyne peeces of grene cloth hanginges, fower foote deep, a Cubberd guilt, too stooles of Crimson velvet and cloth of gold with grene silk frenge, a stoole of cloth of golde & white tuftaffetie with golde frenge, a stoole of cloth of golde tyssued and black tuftaffetie, twentie several pictures, too pictures of mother of pearle too pictures of plaster, twelve pictures of the twelve months, a rownde looking glass, an other glass paynted, an Iron for seacole, a payre of tonges, a payre of virginalls, waynscott rownde about the gallerie. In the lowe dyning Chamber: a long borde to draw out with a frame Carved and inlayde, an other playne borde upon [.......], a foote turkie Carpet, an olde quition of cloth of golde and murry velvet, an iron for seacole, waynscot rownde about the Chamber to the top. At the said dyning Chamber dore a folding bedsted. In my Ladies olde bed Chamber: a bedsted with postes fluted, a tester of yellowe sattin bridges wrought with [...] velvet, bedeshead and single vallans sutable to it with black and yellowe frenge of Cruell, a mattriss, a fetherbed, a bolster, too blanketes, a Coverlet, a Cubberd, a wood Chare, a Close stoole, a Chamber pott, waynscot rownde about the same Chamber to the top. In the utter Chamber to it a bedsted, a sparver paned with cloth of silver and murry velvet imbrodered with letters with silver and murry silk frenge, three Curtins of white and purple taffetie, a quilt of blewe, yellowe and grene taffetie sarcenet, a mattriss, a fetherbed, a lynnen quilt, a bolster, too pillowes, too blanketes, a lyverie Cubberd, a Chare of murry velvet imbrodered with letters and with silk frenge, a little Chare of murry velvet imbrodered with a Twist & with silk frenge, waynscot rownde about that Chamber to the top. In a pallet there a mattriss, a fetherbed, a bolster, a blanket, a Coverlet. In Mr. William Cavendishes Chamber: a borde, waynscot rownde about the Chamber to the top. In the Nurserie waynscot rownde about the top. In the utter Chamber: a little borde, a Cubberd, a Joyned stoole. In the wardrop: a great press, a bedsted, a fetherbed, a bolster, three blanketes, a Coverlet, a borde set upon tressels. In the Chamber over agaynst the wardrop: a bedsted, a fetherbed, too bolsters, too blanketes, a Coverlett, a borde. In the little Chamber at the lowe dyning Chamber dore: a bedsted, a mattriss, a fetherbed, too bolsters, a pillowe, a blanket, a Coverlet, a borde, a Chare. In Mrs Knyvetons Chamber: a bedsted with head and tester sceeled, a fetherbed, too bolsters, a blanket, too Coverletes. In the Corner Chamber uppon the grounde: three bedstedes, too mattrisses, three fetherbedes, fyve bolsters of fethers, too bolsters of wooll, foure blanketes, fyve Coverletes. In the next Chamber to it: too bedstedes, a tester of lynnen, a mattriss, too fetherbedes, foure bolsters, six blanketes, too Coverletes, a table, too wood Chares. In the Chamber over agaynst that Chamber on the grownd: a bedsted, too fetherbedes, too bolsters, too blanketes, a Coverlet, a Counterpoynt of tapestrie, a Cubberd, a borde, a Chare, a holberd. In a Chamber at the side of the hale (the ushers Chamber) too bedstedes, a fetherbed, a bolster, a Coverlet. In a Chamber within that Chamber: a bedsted, a fetherbed, too bolsters, a blanket, too Coverletes, a borde. In the halle: fowre long bordes, seaven formes, an Iron grate for seacole. In a Chamber at the upper end of the halle: a bedsted sceeled over & at the head a pallet Case of straw, a fetherbed, a bolster, a pillowe, too blanketes, a Coverlet, a table, a forme, a holberd, waynscott under the windowe. In the kytchin: Foure long boardes, a brass pott, a lead cestern. In the Larder: a Save of heare to keepe meate in, too tables, tenn shelfes. In the lowe Larder: too bordes. In the pastrie: three long bordes. In the Chamber above the Larder a bedsted. In a Chamber by the Court side: a bedsted, six brass potes, foure brass skellets, a posnet of brass, three brass Chafing dishes, too dripping pans, eight spites, a payre of Cobyrons, eight payre of pothookes, a frying pann, too grates of iron to hold up seacole, a Jack to turn a spit, fyve bowes and a sheaf of arrowes, six Jackes of male, too olde Chestes, a little Iron bounde Cofer, a Chare, a bill, too morters of stone. In too Chambers at the end of the Gallerie the dore opening into the Court: too bedstedes, too fetherbedes, too bolsters, three blanketes, three Coverletes, a bill. In a Chamber in the turret: a bedsted, a mattriss, a fetherbed, a bolster, too blanketes, a Coverlet, a borde. In an other Chamber there: a bedsted, a fetherbed, a bolster, a blanket, a

Coverlet, some Iron teames for waynes. In the other Chamber there: a bedsted, a mattriss, a fetherbed, three bolsters, whereof one of wooll, too blanketes, too Coverletes. In an other Chamber there: too fetherbedes, too bolsters, three blanketes, too Coverletes, & a bedsted. In an other Chamber there: a bedsted, a fetherbed, a bolster, a blanket, too Coverletes. In an other Chamber there: a bedsted, a fetherbed, too bolsters, a Coverlet, a blanket. In an other Chamber there: too bedstedes, fyve mattrisses, fyve bolsters, tenn Coverletes, four blanketes, an Iron bounde Chest. In a Chamber over the backhouse: a bedsted, a fetherbed, a bolster, too blanketes, a Coverlet. In the Backhouse: fowre long bordes, a brass kettle, a trevet, too kites, a kymnell, a kneading trough, a bowlting bing, three tubbes for flower, tenn sackes. In the brewhouse three great Fates, a little fatt, a great bowling lead, a Cooler, eight hogshedes, eight Casting tubs, a tun dishe, two skopes, too firkins. In the wash house fyve tubs. In a Chamber over it a bedsted, a fetherbed, a bolster, too blanketes, too Coverletes, a long table. In the dayrie: a bedsted, a fetherbed, a bolster, three blanketes, a Coverlet, three brass pans, too brass potes, a brandyron, a skellet, too kytes, a Churn, sixe boles, a great trough. In the Slaterhouse: a borde, a brass pot, a flesh axe. In a Chaundlers house: four pans, a trevet, a candletrough of lead, a borde. In the Stable: a bedsted, a fetherbed, too bolsters, a blanket, too Coverletes, three Coches, a Lytter, too payre of Lytter saddles with furniture to them & poles for the Lytters, too gentlewomens saddles, three saddle clothes, three brydells, too pillions, too great buff saddles, a sumpter saddle, too trunck saddles. In a Chamber over the stable, a mattriss, too bolsters, three Coverletes. In Mr. Cavendishes stable, a fetherbed, a bolster, a blanket, too Coverletes. In the Still house Fyve stills of pewter with bottomes of lead. In the Smithie a Slithie, a payre of bellowes.

Notes (by room number)

6 The Forest Great Chamber is at the top of a set of rooms which Bess added to the east end of the Old Hall in the late 1580s. It faced towards the woods behind the house and was decorated above the panelling with trees and deer in three-dimensional coloured plaster work.

14 This grand room is at the top of the extension which Bess added to the west end of the Old Hall. Perched on the edge of the hill, it provides spectacular views on three sides. The elaborate overmantel is flanked by two gigantic figures, probably Gog and Magog, in three-dimensional plasterwork and, above the panelling, the walls are decorated with two rows of plasterwork portals.

19 John Digby was a gentleman servant who married Elizabeth, daughter of Bess's half-sister, Jane Kniveton.

20 William Reason was the receiver at Hardwick; he kept note of the rents and debt repayments due to Bess, which the bailiffs collected

21 The Manners family at Haddon Hall had close links with both Hardwick and Chatsworth. The room may be named after George Manners, who married Grace Pierrepont, daughter of Bess's eldest daughter, Frances Pierrepont.

23 It is not known who Mr Fortescue was; presumably a gentleman servant.

27 The term 'sceeled' reflects the fact that this small room was fully panelled, or sealed, to the ceiling.

34 The nursery had been for William Cavendish's children; see also N.H.47.

40 The ground floor was noted by the clerks as an aid to orientation.

Note:
The 1590 household accounts include some references to repairs in the Embroiderers Chamber and Inner Chamber, although no such rooms occur in the Inventory.

In the newe building at Hardwick

In one of the turretes on the leades: a bedsted with postes turned and Carved and the head inlayde, an other playne bedsted, fowre Iron bounde Chestes, a wood Chest, two trunckes, eleven fetherbedes, newe tickes for fetherbedes, a wooll quilt, three mattrisses, a tapestry Coverlett, five blankettes, three peeces of grene cloth hanginges, too wood Chares, tenn frames for Chares, three wood stooles, a Close stoole covered with lether, an other close stole, a preserving pann of Iron, a warming pann of Iron, a black bill, a sestern of pewter. In an other turret on the leades: twelve

dozen of new pewter dishes, tenn dozen and seaven olde pewter plates, seaven dozen and one sawsers, tenn pewter plates, three pewter boles, three pewter porrengers, three flower potes of pewter, fowre pewter Candlestickes, fowre pewter Chamberpottes, three pans for Close stooles, fowre Candlestickes of brass, Fyftene kettills, eleven pans, three frying pans, too skummers, two morters and pestles, too Chopping knyves, too grydyrons, one dripping pan, a beif forke, too Chafingdishes, Fyftene spittes. In an other Turret at the stayre head; a Clock. In the stayre

Chamber: sixe peeces of guilt lether hanginges, Twelve foote deep, a bedsted with turned postes, a tester and double vallans of blewe cloth sticht with white with blewe and white silk frenge, Fyve Curtins of blewe cloth stitcht with white, a newe Coverlett of blewe cloth, a Cubberd, a Carpet for it of grene cloth stitcht with white & yelloe and black silk frenge, a mattriss, a fetherbed, a bolster, too pillowes, a quilt, too blanketes, a black lether Chare guilded, a quition of tapestry, too Joyned stooles, a Chamber pott, a fyer shovell, a payre of tonges, waynscott under the windowes. In the pallet there, a mattriss, a fetherbed, a bolster, too

blanketes, a Coverlett. In the greene bed Chamber: fowre peeces of tapestrie hanginges with personages, nyne foote deep, a bedsted with head and postes Carved and guilt, a tester with bedes head and double vallans of grene cloth stitcht with yellowe silk and yellowe and grene silk frenge about, Fyve Curtins of grene cloth sticht with yellowe silke, a mattriss, a quilt, a fetherbed, a bolster, too pillowes, a Covering for the bed of newe grene cloth with yellowe and grene silk frenge, and a grene and yellowe lace about it, a quilt of grene sarcenet, too spanishe blanketes, a payre of fusteans, fowre Curtins for the windowes of grene and yellowe tufted sacking, a Cubberd, a turkie Carpet for it, a little folding table, a turkie Carpet for it, a Chare of grene cloth stitcht with yellowe silk, a stoole of grene cloth stitcht with yelloe silke, too Joyned stooles, a close stoole covered with Lether, a stoole pan, a Chamber pott, a payre of Copper Andyrons, a payre of tonges, a fyer shovell, waynscott under the windowes. In a pallet there: a mattriss, a fetherbed, a bolster, too

OF HOUSHOLD STUFF

blankettes, a Coverlet of tapestry. In the Turret Chamber: sixe peeces of 6. Turret chamber hanginges imbrodered uppon white damask murry velvet and other stuffe, Tenn foote deep, a bedsted of white wood with head and postes turned and Carved, a tester bedes head and vallans of black velvet set with stagges and talbottes imbrodered with sivines, with a golde frenge about the vallans, three Curtins wrought with black silk nedlework uppon fine holland Cloth with buttons and lowpes of black silk on the sides. Pantes to goe about the sides of the bed at the bottome of cloth of golde and Crimson velvet, fringed with black and yellowe silk frenge, a Curtin of darnix and a peece of buckerom about the bed to Cover it, fowre Curtins of tufted sacking for the windowes, a mattriss, a fetherbed, a bolster, too pillowes, too spanish blanketes, a payre of fusteans, a grene sarcenet quilt, a Court Cubberd inlayde, a Carpet for it of Cloth of tyssue and black wrought velvet with red and white silk frenge, lyned with Crimson sarcenet, a square table, a Carpet for it of black velvet and white bodkin trymmed with golde, and with white & red silke frenge lyned with black sarcenet, a Chare of cloth of golde and cloth of tyssue, the back nedlework and wrought with golde, a little Chare of cloth of golde, a stoole of cloth of tyssue and black wrought velvet, a Joyned stoole, too Copper Andyrons, a fyer shovell, a payre of tonges, waynscott under the windowes. In the utter Chamber to the Turret Chamber: a bedsted, a matt, 7. Outer chamber to 6 a mattriss, a fether bed, a bolster, too blanketes, a Coverlett, a Cubberd, a little square table, a Joyned stoole, a Close stoole covered with lether, a stoole pan, a Chamber pott. In the servantes Chamber next to the 8. Servants Chamber next to 12 wardrop: too bedstedes, too mattes, too mattrisses, too fetherbedes, too bolsters, fowre blanketes, three Coverletes, a Cubberd with turned postes, a Joyned stoole, too Chamber pottes. In the gallery Chamber: fowre 9. Gallery Chamber peeces of tapestrie hanginges with personages, Eight foote deep, a bedsted with head and postes Carved guilt and inlayde, a tester, bedes head and vallans of Cloth of tyssue lyned with grene buckerom & the vallans having golde and grene solk frenge, three Curtins of Chaungeable taffety, a mattriss, too fetherbedes, a bolster, too pillowes, a payre of fusteans, a quilt, too blanketes, too fledges, a Cover for the bed of wrought silke stuffe red and grene, a Curtin for the windowe of darnix, a Cubberd, a Carpet for it of saye stayned red and white, a nedlework Chare with yellow silk freng, a stoole of cloth of tyssue and Crimson velvet with grene, red, and yellowe silk frenge, too Joyned stooles, a close stoole covered with lether, a stoole pan, a Chamber pott, a payre of Copper Andyrons, a fyer shovell, a payre of tonges, waynscot under the windowe. In a pallet there: a mattriss, a fether bed, a bolster, too blanketes, a tapestry Covering. In the Pearle bed chamber; Fyve peeces of hanginges 10. Pearl Bed-chamber called the planetes, whereof one peece in the wardrop, Eleven foote deep, a bedsted Carved and guilt, a tester bedes head and double vallans of black velvet imbrodered with silver golde and pearle with sivines and woodbines fringed with golde silver and black silk with my Ladies and Sir William Cavendishes Armes in the bedeshead, Fyve Curtins of black and white damask layde about with golde lace and golde frenge, and golde lace downe the middest. A mattriss, a fetherbed, a wooll quilt, a bolster, too pillowes, a payre of fusteans, too spanishe blanketes, a Counterpoynt of black velvet stript with silver, imbrodered with pearle and purle, an other Covering for the bed of black sarcenet quilted, too Curtins for the windowes of darnix, a square table, a Carpet for it of cloth of tyssue and purple wrought velvett, fringed with golde frenge lyned with crimson sattin bridges, A Cubberd, a Carpet for it of nedlework with golde frenge and lyned with red sarcenet, A Chare of cloth of tyssue with golde frenge the frame guilt, a stoole of wrought cloth of golde and silver with yellowe and red silk frenge, a Joyned stoole, a long quition of black velvet imbrodered with golde, silver, and pearle sutable to the bed, the tassells of golde, pearle, black silk and lyned with tuftaffetie. An other quition of purple cloth of silver and golde wrought with black silk frenge and golde & red silke tassells, and lyned with purple velvet, a payre of Copper Andyrons, a fyer shovell, a payre of tonges, a wicker skreyne, waynscott under the windowes. In the pallet there: a mattriss, a fetherbed, a bolster, too blanketes, a Coverlet of fine tapestrie. In a closet by the Pearle bed Chamber: sixe peeces of hanginges of red mockadowe, a Close stoole covered with lether, a stoole pann, a Chamber pott. In the wardrop: a long standing press to laye stuff on with great canvas to Cover it, a tester, bedes head and double vallans of tinsill and black wrought velvet with black silk frenge, a tester for a feild bed of Crimson taffetie sarcenet with red silk frenge, foure Curtins of Crimson taffety sarcenet to it, a Canapie of yellowe saye, stayned with birdes and Antickes, a quilt of Chaungeable taffetie sarcenet. a quilt of yellowe india stuffe imbrodered with birdes and beastes and white silk frenge and tassells, lyned with yellowe sarcenet, too fetherbed tickes of fustean, a Cubberd, a turkie Carpett, a Carpet of yellowe silke and purple Cruell with yellowe and purple silke frenge, and lyned with yellowe buckerom, a saye Carpet rowde yellowe red and blewe, a little Carpett of Cruell Checkered red and yellowe, a long quition of cloth of silver black and white with golde frenge, lyned with yellowe sattin, stript with silver, a long quition of grene cloth of silver with a golde frenge lyned with grene sattin bridges, a long nedlework quition, grounde oringe tawny wrought with knotes with red and blewe silk frenge golde and grene silk buttons lyned with black damask, a long quition of cloth of golde and black stript tuftaffetie, lyned with black sattin bridges, a black velvet quition layde with black silk lace, lyned with black sattin, Eight

OF HOUSHOLD STUFF

square quitions of nedleworke wrought with coulored Cruells, too square quitions of blewe cloth sticht with white, a square quition of red cloth sticht with white, too square quitions of Arras worke, a wood Chare, a stoole of Cloth of golde with yelloe and red silk frenge, too stooles of cloth of silver with red and grene silk frenge, three stooles of cloth of golde and crimson velvet with red and yellowe silk frenge, a stoole of black wrought velvet fringed with yellowe red and grene silke, a stoole of red and grene cloth sticht with white with yellowe and grene frenge, too stooles of grene cloth, too Joyned stooles, a fayre looking glass with paynted glass on the sides, a rownde glass paynted, a frame with armes paynted in it. A table with a mapp, a picture of bastean, fyftene plate Candlestickes of Copper to hang on wales, sixe perfuming panns, too brass Candlestickes, a fayre payre of tables guilt, too peeces of fayre mattes black and white, a wood Chest. In a roome at the wardrop dore: a Curtin of grene saye, an other Curtin of darnix, too Coverletes of tapestry, too blanketes, too copper voyders, nyne payre of beames for imbroderers. In the best bed Chamber: Seaven peeces of hanginges of imbroderie of Cloth of golde and silver, cloth of tyssue, velvett of sondry Coulers, and nedleworke twelve foote deepe, one peece of the picture of fayth and his contrarie Mahomet, an other peece with the picture of hope, and the contrary Judas, an other peece with the picture of temperaunce and the contrary Sardanapales, the other fowre peeces paned and wrought with flowers and slips of nedle-work, a bedsted guilt, a fayre lardge sparver and bedeshead with double vallans of cloth of golde, cloth of silver; sondrie Coulers of velvet imbrodered fayre with divers armes with portalls and pictures, and with a deep golde frenge, sixe Curtins of blewe and red sattin stript with golde and silver and layde with golde lace about the edges and a gold twist downe the seames and fringed about with golde frenge, a mattriss, a downe bed, a downe bolster, too pillowes, a wooll quilt, a payre of fusteans, a white spanishe rugg, a Counterpoynt of Cloth of tyssue paned with cloth of gold and silver and a brode golde lace and golde frenge about it, lyned with Crimson sarcenet, a purple sarcenet quilt, three foote turkie Carpetes the grounde of them white, to laye about the bed, a square table inlayde, a Carpett for it of nedleworke, made with a rose and antickes with a brode golde and silver lace with a border of white sattin imbrodered and a golde frenge, a Cubberd, a Carpet for it of the storie of David and Nathan with trees of needleworke and a border of Crimson velvet about it & golde frenge, A greate Chare trymmed with Crimson velvett imbrodered with golde and with a golde frenge, an other little Chare and a little stoole sutable with a golde frenge, a little Stoole Covered with Crimson velvet imbrodered with nedlework Flowers, too french stooles inlayde sett with marble stones, a Joyned stoole, too nedleworke

13. Room at door of 12

14. Best Bed-chamber

quitions for the windowes, whereof one with my Lord and my ladies Armes wrought in it & lyned with Crimson sattin, the other of Europa wrought with silke golde and silver, and lyned with China Cloth of golde, a quition for the Chare of Crimson velvet imbrodered with pearle with golde frenge about with tassells of silver and yellowe silk and lyned with cloth of silver, a skreyne with a Cover for it of Carnation velvet imbrodered with golde and a golde frenge, a little deske of mother of pearle, a fayre payre of Copper Andyrons, a fier shovell, a payre of tonges, a Close stoole covered with lether, a stool pann, a Chamber pott, waynscott under the windowes. In the servantes Chamber to the best bed Chamber: a bedsted, Carved and guilt, a tester, bedes head and double vallans of grene white and yellowe velvett Cutt and paned with grene silk frenge, fyve Curtins of Carnation taffety, a square table, a mattriss, a fether bed, a bolster, too blanketes, a Covering of tapestrie lyned, a Joyned stoole, a Close Stoole Covered with lether, a stoole pann, a Chamber pott, waynscott rownde about the chamber. In the little Chamber within the best bed-chamber: fyve peeces of hanginges of grene velvet and Cloth of golde and silver set with trees and slips and Ciphers with long borders of stories in nedleworke and borders about all those hanginges of Cloth of tyssue silver and grene silk, everie peece being Eight foote deep, a feild bedsted the postes being covered with black velvet, & layde with three laces of golde and silver lace, a tester, bedes head and vallans of black velvett imbrodered with nedleworke flowers, fringed with golde red blewe and grene silk frenge, fyve guilt knobs to stand on the top of the bed, pantes belowe of the same bed of black velvet imbrodered with flowers, fyve Curtins of Chaungeable damask, a mattriss, a fetherbed, a bolster, too pillowes, a payre of fusteans, too blanketes, a quilt of india stuff imbrodered with beastes with fringe and tassells of white silke, too Curtins for the Windowes of darnix, a square table, a Carpet for it of cloth of tyssue and purple velvet wrought & frenged with yellowe and blewe silk frenge lyned with grene sarcenet, a Cubberd guilt and inlayde, a Carpet for it of blewe velvett imbrodered with nedlework flowers with black and yellowe silk frenge, a Chare of cloth of silver and grene cloth of golde with yellowe silk frenge, a stoole of cloth of golde with yellowe and red silk frenge, an other stoole of cloth of golde and grene velvet, layde with silver lace and silver frenge, too quitions of wrought cloth of golde lyned with yellowe sattin stript with silver & with tassells of golde and with purple and red silke, a Joyned stoole, a payre of Copper Andyrons, a fyer shovell, a payre of tonges, waynscott in the same Chamber rownde about of about fower foote highe. In the passage betwene the best bed Chamber and the gallerie: nyne peeces of hanginges of white cloth with petestalls and portalls of other Coulers and layde with white and yellowe

OF HOUSHOLD STUFF

twyst and with portalls and pavementes rownde about, everie peece twelve foote deep, a great standard, a forme, too Joyned stooles, waynscott rownde about that roome. In the with drawing Chamber: Fyve 18. Withdrawing Chamber peeces of hanginges of Cloth of golde velvett and other like stuffe imbrodered with pictures of the vertues, one of Zenobia, magnanimitas and prudentia, an other of Arthemitia, Constantia and pietas, an other of penelope, prudentia, and sapientia, an other of Cleopatra, fortituto, and Justitia, an other of Lucretia, Charitas and liberalitas, everie peece being twelve foote deep, An other sute of hanginges for the same roome being fowre peeces of Arras of the storie of Abraham, everie peece twelve foote deep. The pictures of the Quene of Scottes, the same Quene and the King of Scotes with theyr Armes both in one, the King and Quene of Scotes hir father & mother in an other, The Erle of Leycester, Sir William Seyntlowe, the prodigall sonne, Marie the Countess of Shrouesbury, Sir Charles Cavendishe, Sir Charles his first wyfe, Ulisses and Penelope, a drawing table Carved and guilt standing uppon sea doges inlayde with marble stones and wood, a Carpet for it of nedleworke of the storie of David and Saule with a golde frenge and trymmed with blewe taffetie sarcenet, a Cubberd with tills Carved and guilt, a Carpet for it of nedleworke with golde frenge lyned with Crimson taffety sarcenet, A nedleworke Chare with golde and grene silk frenge, a footestoole of oring tawnie velvet set with nedleworke slips and oring tawnie frenge, a foote Carpet of turkie worke, a lowe nedleworke stoole with grene yellowe and red silk frenge, Fowre stooles of Crimson velvet imbrodered with nedlework flowers with golde and red silk frenge, too lowe stooles of cloth of golde and silver with grene silk frenge, too lowe stooles of wrought cloth of golde with borders about of nedleworke with golde and silver frenge, too french stooles inlayde and set with marble stones, a little borde inlayde, a little desk of Ibonie, inlayde with white, One long nedlework quition of the storie of Venus and Cupid with blewe silk frenge and tassells, and lyned with blewe damask, an other long quition of nedleworke, the storie of Phaeton with golde frenge, white silke and gold tassells lyned with grene damask, an other long quition of black velvet imbrodered with trees of nedleworke purpled over with golde lyned with black wrought velvett, a payre of Copper Andyrons, a fier shovell, a payre of tonges, waynscott rownde about the same Chamber fowre foote highe. In the high great Chamber: Six peeces of fayre tapestrie hanginges of the 19. High Great Chamber storie of Ulisses Eleven foote deepe, An other sute of hanginges for the same Chamber being eight peeces of woollen cloth stayned with frett and storie and silk flowers, a long table of white wood, a fayre turkie Carpet for the same table, an other fayre long Carpet for it of silk nedlework with gold frenge, lyned with Crimson taffetie sarcenet, an inlayde table in the windowe, a Cubberd guilt and Carved with tills, a Chare of nedlework with golde and silk frenge, a foote Carpet of turkie worke, a footestoole of watchet velvet with blewe silk frenge, three formes Covered with watchet sattin imbrodered with cloth of golde and nedlework flowers with black silk frenge, three other formes Covered with watchet sattin and yellowe velvet with black silk frenge, nyne stooles Covered with nedlework with red, yellowe and white silk frenge, too stooles of white velvet imbrodered with nedlework flowers with white and red silk frenge, three stooles of cloth of golde and cloth of silver with red white and grene silk frenge, too french stooles set with marble stones, Six quitions of cloth of tyssue, three of them purple and three white and yellowe, three quitions of purple velvet with flowers, lyned with hear coulered silk, the Pictures of King Henry the Eight, Quene Elizabeth, Quene Marie, Edward the sixt, Duke Dolva, Charles the Emporer, Cardinal Woolsey, Cardinall Poole, Stephen Gardenner, Fowre pictures of the fowre partes of the worlde, a looking glass paynted about with the Armes of England, waynscott rownde about the Chamber a yarde highe, a wicker skreyne, a payre of brass Andyrons, a fier shovell, a payre of tonges. In the Gallerie: Thirtene peeces of deep Tapestrie hanginges of the storie of Gedion everie peece being nyntene foote deep, too square inlayde tables, too fayre turkie Carpets for them the fretes Carnation and white & bordered about, too other nedlework Carpetes for them, one with my Ladies Armes in the middest with a deep golde frenge about and lyned with red sarcenet, the other with my Lord and my Ladies Armes in the middest with a deep golde frenge aboute & lyned with red taffetie sarcenet, a Chare of nedleworke with a golde and silver bonelace and silver and Crimson silk frenge, a Chare of nedleworke with golde and grene silk frenge, an other Chare of nedelworke with yellowe and blewe silk frenge, a footestoole of watchet velvet, a foote Carpet of turkie worke, a lowe stoole of black and grene velvett & cloth of golde with golde lace and with golde and silver frenge, a lowe stoole of cloth of golde and cloth of silver with grene and yellowe silk frenge, a lowe stoole of nedleworke with blewe and white silk frenge, a forme covered with Crimson and white damask with yellow and grene silk frenge, a forme Covered with grene velvet and white sattin stayned, nyntene long quitions whereof one for the Chare the rest for the windowes viz: one long quition for the Chare the grounde purple velvett imbrodered with golde and silver with a portall and beastes, birdes and flowers with silver and black silk frenge, oring tawnie silk and silver tassells lyned with purple velvett, the rest for the windowes, viz: one long quition the grounde purple velvet, the fancie of a fowler and other personages in nedleworke with blewe silk frenge & tassells & lyned with blewe damask, one other long quition of silke Crosstitch, blewe and yellowe billetes the grounde tawnie with blewe silk frenge and tassells and lyned with blewe damask, another long quition of silk bred stitch the fret grene, the grounde red with black silk and silver frenge, tassells of red silk and silver lyned with red and yellowe stitcht taffetie, too other long quitions of Crimson sattin imbrodered with Straweberries and wormes with blewe silk frenge and tassells & lyned with blewe damaske, an other long quition of nedlework the grounde Crosstitcht of watchet silk with flowers, strawberries and oke leaves fringe & tassells of grene silk and silver lyned with watchet velvet, an other long quition of nedleworke of the storie of Acteon and Diana with golde frenge grene silk and silver tassells lyned with grene Damaske, an other long quition of Crimson velvett, a frett of cloth of silver with slips of nedleworke in it, frenge and tassells of golde and Crimson silk lyned with oringe tawnie sattin. An other long quition of petepoynt wrought with silk of the storie of Atalanta with blewe silk frenge and tassells lyned with blewe damask, an other long quition of grene velvett set with slips of nedleworke with grene and yellowe silke frenge, grene silke and gold tassells, lyned with cloth of silver white grene and yellowe, An other long quition of crimson velvet set with slips of nedleworke with grene red and yellowe silk frenge, tassells of Crimson silke and golde, lyned with Crimson velvett, An other long quition of nedlework grounded white, a pear tree and slips, frenge and tassells of blewe silke, & lyned with blewe and yellowe damaske, An other long quition of Cross stitch with flowers, the grounde white, the fret grene set with slips with freng tassells and bottome of blewe silke. An other long quition of nedleworke ground Crimson set with slips with blewe silke frenge & tassells, lyned with blewe damask, An other long quition of nedleworke of hunting the hare, the fringe and tassells of blewe silk & lyned with blewe damaske, an other long quition of nedleworke of the platt of Chatesworth house with grene red and yellowe silke frenge buttons of Carnation silke and silver & lyned with white grene and yellowe cloth of silver, An other long quition of nedleworke, silk & Cruell of the storie of the sacryfice of Isack with frenge and tassells of blewe silk & lyned with blewe damaske, an other long quition of nedleworke, silke & Cruell of the storie of the Judgment of Saloman betwene the too women for the Childe, with frenge and tassells of blewe silk and lyned with blewe damask, pillowes to all those quitions stufte with fethers, fowre square quitions of Arras worke. The Pictures of Quene Elizabeth, Edward the second, Edward the third, Rychard the third, Henry the fourth, Henry the fyft, Henry the sixt, Edward the fourth, Rychard the third, Henry the seaventh, Henry the Eight, Edward the sixt, Quene Marie, Quene Elizabethes picture in a less table, The King of Fraunce, Henry, King of Scottes, James, King of Scottes, The picture of Our Ladie the Virgin Marie, Quene Anne, Henry, the third King of

Fraunce in a little table, The Duke of Bullen, Phillip, King of Spayne, Twoo twynns, Quene Katherin, The Erle of Southampton, Mathewe, Erle of Lenox, Charles, Erle of Lenox, George, Erle of Shrouesbury, My Ladie, Lord Bacon, The Marquess of Winchester, the Ladie Arbella, Mr Henry Cavendishe, The Lord Straunge, The Lord Cromwell, Mrs Ann Cavendishe, The Duke of Sommerset, Sir Thomas Wyet, The storie of Joseph, a looking glass with a border of imbroderie, a looking glass set with mother of pearle and silver, a table of Iverie carved and guilt with little pictures in it of the natyvitie, a buckler of silver and guilt the middest set with stones, of the storie of Hercules, lyned with Crimson velvet and with golde and Crimson silk frenge, a peece of watchet velvet to hang betwixt it and the wale, the picture of hell, a skreyne, a Cloth for the skreyne of Crimson velvet with a brode perchment lace of golde through the middest & rownde about and with a golde frenge about lyned with Crimson taffetie sarcenet, a payre of great Copper Andyrons, too fier shovells, too payre of tonges, waynscott under the windowes. In the

Shipp bed Chamber: Fyve peeces of tapestrie hanginges with personages whereof one in the wardrop Tenn foote deep, the ship bedsted Carved and guilt, a tester and bedes head of red cloth with black lace and black silk frenge, fowre Curtins of red cloth with black lace, an other tester of lynnen cloth wrought with silke of divers Coulers with a brode parchment lace of golde and a golde frenge about it, fowre Curtins and bedes head of lynnen cloth wrought sutable to the same, a mattriss, a fetherbed, a bolster, too pillowes, too blanketes, a payre of fusteans, a Counterpoynt of imbroderie and nedleworke with Cloth of golde and divers other stuffes and with a golde frenge, a Counterpoynt of red Cloth with yellowe silke frenge, a marble table, a Cubberd guilt and inlayde, too Chares of red cloth with red silk frenge, a stoole of red cloth with red silk frenge, a Joyned stoole, a long quition of cloth of silver imbrodered & with grene and yellowe silk frenge and lyned with stript sattin, an other quition of cloth of golde of both sides, too Curtins of damask and sarcenet for the windowes, too Curtins of darnix for the windowes, a payre of Copper Andyrons, a fyer shovell, a payre of tonges, a Close stoole, a stoole pann, a Chamber pott, waynscott under the windowes. In a little Closet there: a

mattriss, a fetherbed, a bolster, too blanketes, a Coverlet of tapestrie, a Joyned stoole. In Tobies Chamber: Fyve peeces of tapestrie hanginges

of the storie of Tobie Tenn foote deep, a bedsted with head and postes covered with Cloth of golde, cloth of silver and oring coulored velvet, a tester of oring & murry coulored velvet imbrodered with golde and silver twist, double vallans of murry and tawnie velvett, with golde, silver and silk frenge, all imbrodered with twyst and the seames layde on with bone lace and armes in the bedes head, fyve Curtins of yellowe and red damaske layde with parchment lace of golde and silke over the seames, a mattriss, a downe bed, a fetherbed, a downe bolster, too pillowes, a diaper quilt, a payre of fusteans, too spanishe blanketes, a red sarcenet quilt, a Counterpoynt paned with cloth of golde and murry wrought velvet, too darnix Curtins for the windowes, a Court Cubberd inlayde, a Carpet for it of fine turkie worke, a square table inlayde, a Carpet for it of fine turkie worke, too Chares and a stoole of murry and yellowe velvet with murry silke and golde frenge, a little inlayde stoole, a Joyned stoole, a long quition of Cloth of golde and Crimson velvet with silver and red silk buttons & frenge lyned with washcoulored bridges sattin, a long quition of murry and oring coulored velvet imbrodered with golde twist with silke and silver buttons and lyned with washcoulored sattin bridges, a payre of Copper Andyrons, a fier shovell, a payre of tonges, a skreyne of buckerom, a Close stoole inlayde, a stoole pann, a Chamber pott, waynscott under the windowes. In a pallet there: a mattriss, a fetherbed, a bolster, too blanketes, a tapestrie Coverlett. In Jacobs Chamber: too peeces of tapestrie hanginges with personages twelve foote deep, a bedsted with postes Carved and head inlayde, a tester, bedes head and vallans of blewe cloth layde with black silk lace and the vallans with black silk frenge, fyve Curtins of blewe cloth with black silk knottes, a mattriss, a fether bed, a bolster, a pillowe, too blanketes, a quilt of yellowe and red Cruell, a little Table, a Carpett of grene cloth with a black garde of velvet Cutt and black and yellow frenge, a wood Chare, a stoole covered with murry velvet, & with yellowe silk frenge, a Joyned stoole, a tapestrie quition, a map with a frame, a close stoole covered with lether, a stoole pann, a Chamber pott, a payre of Iron Andyrons, a fier Shovell, a payre of tonges, waynscot under the windowe. In a pallet there: a mattriss, a fetherbed, a bolster, too blanketes, a Coverlett. In the half pace at the stare head: a long drawing table, a Cubberd, Fyve formes, a great glass Lanthorne. In the upper Chapple: too peeces of hanginges imbrodered with pictures Seaven foote and a half deep, three inlayde formes, a Chare of grene cloth of silver and white unshorne velvet with a golde frenge, a stoole of cloth of golde with a little golde frenge, fowre quitions of grene damask lyned with russet sattin bridges, one long quition of Cloth of golde & Cloth of silver lyned with blewe sattin bridges, an other long quition of Cloth of golde & red damaske lyned with wash Coulored sattin bridges, an other long quition of cloth of golde and white unshorne velvet lyned with blewe sattin bridges, an other long quition of black wrought velvet lyned with murry sattin bridges, a quition of turkie worke, a foote turkie Carpet, waynscott rownde about the Chapple. In the lowe Chapple: a Pulpitt, a Cubberd, fowre formes, a Crucefixe of imbrodered worke, too pictures of our Ladie the Virgin Marie and the three Kinges, the salutation of the Virgin Marie

24. Jacob's Chamber

25. Landing
26. Upper Chapel

27. Lower Chapel

by the Angle. In the little dyning Chamber, a long drawing table, a turkie Carpet for it, a Chare of turkie worke, a stoole of turkie worke, fowrtene Joyned stooles, a fyer shovell, a payre of tonges, waynscott rownde about the same roome. In the lowe great Chamber: Eight peeces of tapestrie hanginges of the storie of David Eleven foote deep, a long table Carved and inlayde, too long turkie Carpetes for it, a square table set with marble stones & inlayde with black and white wood, an other square table, a square turkie Carpet for it, a Cubberd, too turkie Carpetes for it, one of them with my Ladies Armes in it, a Chare of Cloth of golde and silver with a frett of grene velvet and with grene silk frenge, a Chare of murry and yelloe velvet with golde and red silk frenge, a Chare of yellowe sattin bridges imbrodered over with russet velvet with yellowe and black silk frenge, too little Chares of Crimson velvet with golde frenge, a footestoole of wood, a foote Carpet of turkie worke, Eight stooles of black and white Carsey imbrodered with nedleworke Flowers with red and black silk frenge, a lowe stoole of Cloth of golde and silver with a fret of grene velvett and with a grene silke frenge, a little inlayde stoole, too formes of Cloth of gold with a border of grene velvet and golde frenge, a forme of cloth of silver with a border of grene velvet and golde frenge, a forme of yellowe damaske with a border of Crimson velvet and golde frenge, one long quition of Cloth of golde with a golde frenge and lyned with russet sattin, an other long quition of Clothe of golde and silver fretted with grene velvet, lyned with yelloe sattin bridges, an other long quition of cloth of golde and black velvett stript with silver lyned with black damaske, too other long quitions of Cloth of golde and Crimson velvet set with spangles of silver and with silver frenge and tassells of golde and silver and red silk lyned with washcoulored sattin, an other quition of white sattin imbrodered with a golde twist lyned with white sattin, an other long quition of Cloth of silver and grene velvet, with a rose imboste in the middest with a golde lace and a golde frenge lyned with wash-coulored sattin bridges, too Curtins of grene penistone for the windowes, a wicker skreyne, the pictures of Quene Elizabeth, George, Erle of Shrouesbury, A glass with his and my Ladies Armes in it, the Lord Burleigh, Lord Tresorer, The Ladie Margaret, Countess of Lenox, Charles, Erle of Lenox, her sonne, The Ladie Arbella her grandChilde, My Ladies picture, Sir William Cavendishe, Mr. William Cavendishe the elder, Mr. William Cavendishe the younger, The Virgin Marie, Mr. Thomas Cavendishe, father to Sir William Cavendishe, twelve tables with Armes set in them, a payre of Copper Andyrons, an Iron Chymney, a fier shovell, a payre of tonges, waynscot under the windowes. Over the skreyne in the halle a greate standerd Covered with lether, a Chare of black lether and some guilt, a stoole inlayde, a great frame with Armes, a holberd, wayscotted under the windowes and at the endes, a tarras over the skreyne. In my Ladies with drawing Chamber: six peeces of tapestrie hanginges with personages and my Ladies Armes in them, wayscott under the hainginges rownde about, the hanginges Sixe foote deep, an inlayde borde, too grene cloth Carpetes for it, a Cubberd Carved guilt and inlayde, a great inlayde Chest, a Chare of black lether guilded, a footestoole of wood, a foote turkie Carpet, a little Chare of wrought cloth of gold with golde and red silk frenge, a Chare of turkie worke, too Chares for Children, fyve stooles of turkie worke, a little stoole of grene cloth, too black lether stooles, three inlayde stooles, too inlayde formes, too long quitions of Cloth of golde and red damask, one of them lyned with russet velvet, the other with washcoulored sattin bridges, a quition of silk nedle-worke for the Chare, a quition of nedleworke of Cruell, a long quition of unshorne Crimson velvet, a long quition of Crimson velvett, a turkie Carpet, a Travice like a skreyne covered with violet Coulored Cloth layde about with black lace, a wood skreyne, a Cover for it of grene Cloth, a wicker skreyne, three truncks, a great Chest with tills, an Iron bounde Chest, too Curtins of darnix for the windowes, my Ladies picture, a glass with my Ladies Armes, a mapp, three tables with armes in them, a payre of Copper Andyrons, an Iron Chymney with a back of Iron, a fyer shovell, a payre of tonges. In my Ladies Bed Chamber: too peeces of tapestrie hanginges with personages and forrest worke Fyftene foote and a half deep, a bedsted, the postes being Covered with scarlet layd on with silver lace, bedes head, tester and single vallans of scarlet, the vallans imbrodered with golde studes and thissells, stript downe and layde about with golde and silver lace and with golde frenge about, three Curtins of scarlet stript downe with silver lace and with silver and red silk buttons and lowpes, fyve Curtins of purple bayes, a mattriss, a fetherbed, a bolster, a pillowe, too little pillowes, too quiltes whereof one lynnen, the other diaper, three payre of fusteans, Six spanish blanketes, eight fledges about the bed, too Curtins of red Cloth for the windowes, three Coverletes to hang before a windowe, a Coverlett to hang before a Dore, a Counterpoynt of tapestrie before an other dore, a Cubberd inlayde and Carved, a little folding table, a turkie Carpet to it, a Chare of russet sattin stript with silver & with silver and russet silk frenge, too foote-stooles of wood, too foote Carpetes of turkie worke, a Covering for the russet sattin Chare of scarlet imbrodered with flowers of petepoynt, a stoole and a footestoole of scarlet sutable to the same, a highe Joyned stoole, too other Joyned stooles, an inlayde stoole, a long quition of cloth of golde on both sides, a long quition of nedlework of Cruel with pances and lyned with grene says, a little nedlework quition with my Ladies Armes in it lyned with red velvet, my Ladies bookes viz: Calvin uppon Jobe, Covered with

31. My Lady's Withdrawing Chamber

32. My Lady's Bed-chamber

russet velvet, the resolution, Salomans proverbes, a booke of meditations, too other bookes Covered with black velvet, a looking glass, an hower glass, too brushes, a payre of pullies lyned with black taffetie, a great Iron Chest paynted, three great trunckes, too little trunckes, three Deskes Covered with lether whereof one a great one, a lyttle deske to write on guilded, a little Cofer guilt, a little Cofer covered with lether, a little Cofer covered with black velvet, three flatt Cofers covered with lether, a boxe paynted and guilded with my Lordes and my Ladies Armes on it, a Yellowe Cotten to Cover it, an other boxe Covered with grene velvet, too trussing Cofers bounde with Iron, fyve wood boxes, a wicker skreyne, a payre of Copper Andyrons, a payre of Iron Andyrons, a fyer shovell, a payre of tonges, a payre of bellowes, My Ladie Arbells bedsted, a Canapie of darnix blewe and white with guilt knobs and blewe and white frenge, a Cloth of Checker work of Cruell about the bed, a mattriss, a fetherbed, a bolster, a quilt, four spanishe blanketes, a payre of fusteans. In a pallet there: a mattriss, a fetherbed, too bolsters, too blanketes, a Coverlett, waynscott under the windowes. In a little roome within my Ladies Chamber: a Close stoole covered with blewe cloth stitcht with white, with red and black silk frenge, three pewter basons, a little Close stoole, a great Cofer, a wood Chest, a great trunck, a little trunck. In the Maydes Chamber: a square table, foure Iron bounde Cofers, nyne trunckes, a wood Chest, too wood deskes, too wood boxes, sixtene poundes brass waightes habberdepoiz, a payre of ballans, a pownde of brass waightes troye waight, a little payre of ballans, a wood skreyne, a payre of Iron Andyrons, a fier shovell, a payre of tonges, a lead waight. In the Closet within the Maydes Chamber: a borde, a Chare covered with lether and guilt, a great Standerd, a great Iron bounde Cofer, a wood Cofer, trunckes. At my Ladies Chamber dore a Trunck, and in a pallet there a mattriss, a fetherbed, a bolster, a blanket, too Coverletes. In my ladie Arbells Chamber: six peeces of hanginges of yellowe, blewe and other Coulored damask and sattin wrought with golde flowers and trees and lyned with Canvas, a bedsted, a mattriss, a downe bed, a wooll quilt, a bolster, a pillowe, a payre of fusteans, three spanishe blankettes, a white fledge, a Canapie of Chaungeable taffetie laced and fringed with white and red silk, three Curtins of the same stuffe to it, a Cubberd, a Carpet for it of nedleworke wrought with antickes and frettes, with grene silke frenge and lyned with watchet sarcenet, a square table, a Carpet for it of russet velvet paned with golde and silver lace and layde with golde and silver lace and Frenge about lyned with yelloe and grene sattin bridges, a long narrowe quition of silk needlework wrought with leaves, and knotes with red silk fringe and lyned with black sattin bridges, an other long quition of silke nedleworke wrought with knottes with yellowe red and grene silk frenge

OF HOUSHOLD STUFF

and lyned with black Damask, tenn peeces of Darnix, a Joyned stoole, a fier shovell, a payre of tonges, waynscott under the windowes. In the utter roome there: a mattriss, too fetherbedes, too bolsters, a pillowe, too blanketes, a Coverlet. At my Ladies with Drawing Chamber Dore, a bedsted to turne up like a Chest, a mattriss, a fetherbed, a bolster, too blanketes, a Coverlet, a Cubberd, too joyned stooles, three holberdes, a Candlestick of wood paynted and guilded with birdes. In the great half pace next above that: too bedstedes to turne up like Chestes, too mattrisses, too fetherbedes, too bolsters, fowre blanketes, too Coverletes, a square table, foure Joyned formes, a great standerd, a holberd, a great glass Lanthorne. In the gentlewomens Chamber: a bedsted, a mattriss, a fetherbed, a bolster, too blanketes, a Coverlett, a Cubberd, a Joyned stoole. In a Closet within that Chamber: an Iron bounde Cofer, too trunckes. In Prodigall Chamber: three peeces of tapestrie hanginges of the storie of the Prodigall sonne, Eleven foote deep, a feild bedsted Carved and guilt, a tester of Cloth of tyssue lyned with yellow taffetie and single vallans of the same stuff with golde and silver frenge, the bedes head of blewe and yellowe damaske layde with golde lace, fyve Curtins of blewe and yellowe damask layd with golde and silver lace and golde frenge, a mattriss, a fetherbed, a bolster, too pillowes, a wooll quilt, a payre of fusteans, the picture of the Lady Elizabeth Talbott, a Cubberd guilt and inlayde with a marble stone in the side, a little table inlayde, a Chare of Crimson velvett layde with golde and silver lace and with golde frenge, a stoole of Cloth of golde with silver frenge, a Joyned stoole, a payre of brass Andyrons, a fier shovell, a payre of tonges, waynscott under the windowes. In a little Closet there: a mattriss, a fetherbed, a bolster, too blankets, a Coverlet, a Close stoole, a stoole pann, a Chamber pott. In Mr. William Cavendishe's Chamber: Fyve peeces of tapestrie hanginges of Forrest work nyne foote deep, a bedsted, a tester, bedes head and single vallans of blewe cloth sticht with white with blewe and white silk frenge, fyve Curtins of blewe cloth sticht with white thred, a mattriss, a downe bed, a fetherbed, three bolsters, a pillowe, a wolle quilt, a payre of fusteans, three blankets, a fledg, too peeces of darnix, a Cubberd, a Carpet to it of grene cloth, a folding table, a Carpet to it of grene cloth, a Chare of blewe cloth stitcht with white, with yellowe and grene silk frenge, three joyned stooles, a wycker skreyne, a payre of Iron Andyrons, a fier shovell, a payre of tonges, too Chamber pottes, a holberd, waynscott under the windowes. In a pallet there: a mattriss, a fetherbed, too bolsters, too blanketes, a Coverlett. In the Chamber at the end of the walke: a bedsted, with head and postes Carved, a tester of red and grene buckerom, a tester of red and grene saye fringed, an olde Curtin of red and grene saye, too mattrisses, too fetherbedes, three bolsters, three pillowes, seaven

38. Outer room to 37

39. At door to 31

40. Half-landing

41. Gentlewomen's Chamber

42. Closet in 41

43. Prodigal Chamber

44. Small closet in 43

45. Mr William Cavendish's Chamber

46. Chamber at end of Walk

blankettes, a fledge, a Coverlet, a Coverlet of tapestrie, too wood Chares, a quition of Coverlet worke, a quition of lystes, a Close stoole, a stoole pann, a Chamber pott, a borde. In the Nurserie: too mattrisses, too fetherbedes being little ones, too other fetherbedes, too fledges, too bolsters too pillowes, sixe blankettes, too Coverletes, a Cubberd, a folding table, a square table, a wood chare, a payre of Iron Andyrons, a Close stoole. In Mrs. Knyvetons Chamber: seaven peeces of darnix hangings, a bedsted, a Canapie of cloth of golde and murry velvet, too buckerom Curtins, a green Cloth Curtin, a Curtin of red and grene saye, a mattriss, too fetherbedes, a quilt, too bolsters, a pillowe, a fustean, too blanketes, a Coverlet, a Cubberd, a Carpet of rowde stuffe of Cruell, a Joyned stoole, a quition of nedleworke, a quition of turkie worke, a payre of tonges, a Close stoole. In a pallet there: a mattriss, a fetherbed, a bolster, a blanket, too Coverletes. In a Chamber betwene the pantrie and the Nurserie: too bedstedes, too mattrisses, too fetherbeds, too bolsters, fowre blanketes, too Coverletes. In the hale: Foure peeces of tapestrie hanginges with personages of forrest worke of fyftene foote and a half deep, wayscott under the same hanginges and rownde about the hale, three long tables, sixe formes, too great Copper Candlestickes with severall places to set lightes in hanging in too ropes paynted, foure plate Candlestickes of brass to hang on the wales, a great Iron back for a Chymney. In a little roome betwene the Chapple and the hale: a bedsted, a mattriss, a fetherbed, a bolster, a blanket, a Coverlet. In the Pantrie: a Cubberd, a long Table, two little Tables, an Ironbounde Chest, a great wood Chest, a trunck, a forme, a wood Chare, too Joyned stooles, too Binges for bread, foure brass Candlestickes, a tub to wash plate in, a twiggen basket. In a Chamber within the Pantrie: a bedsted, a mattriss, a fetherbed, too bolsters, three blanketes, a Coverlet, too holberdes. In the Butterie and Sellors: too pewter Sesterns, fyve Settees, thirtie and three hogshedes, too tubs, a Charcole pan, foure black lether Jackes, a payre of slinges, too Cases of bottles covered with seyle skins, a plate Candlestick. In the wyne Sellours: foure settles, twentie and one hogshedes, a butt of Sack, too firkins. In the kitchin: Foure long bordes, a long pewter pott, twelve dozen and Sixe pewter dishes, to dozen Sawsers, twelve pewter plates, a pie plate of pewter, sixe brass potes, twoo brass posnetes, a great Copper pann. In the boyling house: three brass panns, a brass kettle, a morter and pestle of brass, a plate Candlestick of brass, a frying pann, a Coliander, a Chopping knife, a mincing knyfe, a Cleyver, a grydyron, a grater, tenn spites, Fyve dripping panns, a skummer, a hatchet. In the little kitchin: three bordes. In the drie Larder: three bordes, a Cubberd, too shelfes, a wood Chare. In the lowe Larder: too Sesterns of lead, three bordes, foure tubs, a hogshead, too shelfes. In the Pastrie: a borde. In the Skullerie: a mattriss, a bolster, a blanket, three Coverletes. In the surveying place at the kitchin dore: three bordes. In the little turret at the south side of the Court: a bedsted, a fether bed, three blanketes, a Coverlet, a peece of darnix, a Cubberd. In the Porters Lodg: too fetherbedes, a bolster, too blanketes, a Coverlet, a borde, too holberdes.

63. Surveying Place at Kitchen Door; 64. Small turret

65. Porter's Lodge

Plate in the saide newe building as followeth, viz: a Cupp of Angle golde with a Cover waying sixtene ounces and a quarter, a Cup of french Crowne golde, with a Cover waying nyne ounces three quarters, a Sault of golde with a Cover waying fowre ounces, an other Salt of golde and Christall enameled with a Cover and with a talbott on the top and stages beneath and with a Scutchion of my Lord and my Ladies Armes, waying Fyve ounces and a half, a spoone of golde with a talbott and my Lord and my Ladies armes on the end and my Lordes armes on the backside waying too ounces three quarters. A fayre guilt bason and Ewre enamild and wrought and waying one hundreth thirtie foure ounces three quarters, an other fayre guilt bason and Ewre wrought waying one hundreth thirtie nyne ounces three quarters, an other fayre guilt bason and Ewre wrought waying one hundreth fyftie foure ounces three quarters, an other guilt bason and Ewre waying fowrscore tenn ounces and a half, an other guilt bason and Ewre waying threescore too ounces and a half, an other bason and Ewre parcell guilt waying Fourscore and eight ounces, an other bason and Ewre parcell guilt waying fourscore & one ounces, an other bason and Ewre parcell guilt waying threescore eight ounces and a half, another Bason and Ewre white waying threescore too ounces & a half, an other bason and Ewre white, waying Fortie six ounces and a half, A great deep bason white waying fyftie one ounces & a half, an other deep bason white waying thirtie fyve ounces, an other deep bason white, waying twentie nyne ounces, an other deep bason white, waying nyntene ounces and a half, a white Ewre for wine with a Cover waying nyntene ounces & a half, a whyte Ewre without a Cover waying nyntene ounces and a half, too little white Ewres with Covers waying twelve ounces, a little Christall Salt with a Cover trymmed with silver and guilt waying seventene ounces, A great guilt salt with a Cover & pictures waying threescore too ounces, a great guilt salt with a Cover and tills waying Fourscore six ounces, a little broken salt with a ramme guilt & wrought waying nyne ounces, a double bell salt with a Cover & a pepper boxe guilt waying twelve ounces quarter, an other guilt salt with a Cover waying twentie too ounces three quarters, an other guilt salt with a Cover waying sixtene ounces quarter; an other guilt salt with a Cover waying fyftene ounces, an other guilt salt with a Cover waying seventene ounces quarter, an other guilt salt with a Cover waying nyne ounces & a half, an other guilt salt with a Cover waying sixtene ounces, an other guilt salt with a Cover waying fowre

Plate

ounces, an other salt with a Cover white waying fowre ounces and a half, Too lyverie potes with Covers guilt waying Fyftie fyve ounces & a half, too other lyverie potes with Covers guilt waying threescore seaven ounces and a half, too other lyverie potes with Covers guilt waying One hundreth three ounces, Too lyverie potes with Covers parcell guilt waying too hundreth threescore nine ounces and a quarter, an other payre of lyverie potes parcell guilt waying fourscore six ounces, an other payre of lyverie potes parcell guilt waying three score eight ounces. A great lyverie pott parcell guilt waying threescore eleven ounces, too long lyverie potes white waying One hundreth fyftie too ounces, too other lyverie potes white waying three score fyve ounces, a posset pot with a Cover white waying twentie six ounces & a half, a posset pott without a Cover white waying twentie three ounces, too tankerdes guilt with Covers waying thirtie fyve ounces, too tankerdes white with Covers waying fortie fyve ounces and a half, a little guilt Jugg with a Cover waying Eleven ounces, an other little guilt Jugg without a Cover waying sixtene ounces, a guilt Cann graven with a Cover waying sixtene ounces, a mawdlin Cup with a Cover guilt waying thirtene ounces, too Jugges with Covers parcell guilt waying fortie ounces, a little Jugg with a Cover parcell guilt waying nyne ounces and a quarter. my Ladies Cup with a Cover white waying thirtene ounces, a white Jugg with a Cover with my Ladies Armes waying Eightene ounces, an olde white Jugg without a Cover waying Eightene ounces. A great guilt standing Cup like a goard with a Cover waying Fortie too ounces, an other standing Cup with a Cover guilt waying fortie one ounces and a half, an other standing Cup with a Cover guilt waying fortie ounces. An other standing Cup with a Cover guilt waying fortie one ounces, an other standing Cup with a Cover guilt waying thirtie one ounces, an other standing Cup with a Cover guilt waying thirtie one ounces, an other standing Cup with a Cover guilt waying thirtie fyve ounces and a half, an other standing Cup with a Cover guilt waying twentie six ounces, a standing Cup without a Cover guilt waying seventene ounces, a pursland Cup with a Cover trymmed with silver and guilt waying fourtene ounces, a great guilt bole with a Cover waying thirtie foure ounces, an other guilt bole with a Cover waying fortie one ounces quarter, an other guilt bole with a Cover waying nyntene ounces and a half, an other guilt bole with a Cover waying thirtene ounces & a half, an other guilt bole with a Cover waying twentie six ounces and a half, an other guilt bole with a Cover waying thirtie ounces, an other guilt bole with a Cover waying twentie nyne ounces. An other guilt bole with a Cover waying eightene ounces & a quarter, an other guilt bole with a Cover waying twentie fyve ounces, an other guilt bole with a Cover waying thirtie ounces & a half, another guilt bole with a Cover waying nyntene ounces & a half, an other guilt bole with a Cover waying eightene ounces & a half, an other guilt bole with a cover waying twentie fyve ounces & a half, an other guilt bole with a cover waying twelve ounces, an other guilt bole with a Cover waying thirtie ounces & a half, a guilt bole without a Cover waying eightene ounces & a half, an other guilt bole without a Cover waying seventene ounces & a quarter, another guilt bole without a Cover waying fourtene ounces & three quarters, an other guilt bole without a Cover waying sixtene ounces, an other guilt bole without a Cover waying nyne ounces, a guilt Chaced bole without a Cover waying nyne ounces, two Covers for boles guilt waying thirtene ounces three quarters. A white bole with a Cover waying fourtene ounces three quarters, a white bole without a Cover waying eightene ounces & a half, an other white brode bole without a Cover waying eightene ounces, an other white bole without a Cover waying fyftene ounces, an other white bole without a Cover waying thirtene ounces, an other white bole without a Cover waying twelve ounces, an other white bole without a Cover waying tenn ounces, an other white bole without a Cover wayinge eleven ounces & a half, an other white mounsers bole without a Cover waying twelve ounces. A Case of six tonnes, too saltes, & a peper boxe parcell guilt waying three score nyntene ounces & a half, a Case of fyve tonnes with a Cover, a salt and a pepper boxe white waying threescore and nyne ounces, A tun or mawdlin Cup parcell guilt without a Cover waying seven ounces and a half. A Case of plate with too Ewres, a pepper boxe and a salt guilt waying threescore tenn ounces & a quarter. Too trenchers of estate guilt with a spoone, toothpikes and a little tune dishe waying three score six ounces and a half, Foure guilt plates waying twentie & seven ounces, twentie and three plates parcell guilt with my Ladies armes, waying too hundreth twentie foure ounces and a half, twelve other plates parcell guilt waying fourscore & thirtene ounces, nyne plates with talbotes white waying threescore fourtene ounces, foure other white plates waying thirtie too ounces and a half, thirtie and one guilt spoones waying thirtie eight ounces, thirtie and sixe other spoones whereof eleven with knobs and nyne with thappostles waying fyftie one ounces & a half, too great platters parcell guilt waying fourscore twelve ounces, sixe other platters parcell guilt with my Ladies Armes waying one hundreth threescore fourtene ounces, sixe other platters parcell guilt waying too hundreth and seventene ounces. Twentie and too dishes parcell guilt with my Ladies Armes waying Foure hundreth and fortie ounces, twelve other dishes parcell guilt waying three hundreth and fourtene ounces, twelve lesser dishes parcell guilt waying twoo hundreth fortie too ounces. Eight white dishes waying three hundreth twentie foure ounces, too other dishes white waying threescore fyve ounces, three deep little dishes white waying fyftie eight ounces & a half, twoo long dishes white waying threescore sixtene ounces and a half. Eleven sawsers parcell guilt with my Ladies Armes waying fourscore eleven ounces & a half, a guilt porrenger with a Cover waying fourtene ounces & a half, an other guilt porrenger with a Cover waying fourtene ounces and a halfe, a white porrenger without a Cover waying nyne ounces & a quarter, an other white porrenger without a Cover waying nyne ounces & a half, a suger boxe white waying twentie nyne ounces and a half, an other sugar boxe white waying twentie too ounces, a posnet white waying thirtie too ounces & a half, a skellet white waying Fortie seven ounces, a great pott white to boyle thinges in waying threescore eight ounces, an other less pot to boyle thinges in waying thirtie seven ounces & a half, a grydyron white waying twentie ounces and a half, a frying pan waying fyftie eight ounces and a half, a pan to boyle thinges in white waying threescore fyftene ounces, a Chafer for water white waying fourscore one ounces, a bucket without a Cover white waying nyntene ounces & a half, a pestle and morter white waying fortie ounces, a basket for fruit white waying nyntene ounces and a half, too Flaggons guilt waying one hundreth fourscore eleven ounces, too lyttle flaggons guilt waying twentie eight ounces, too Flagons white waying one hundreth sixtene ounces, a Casting bottle guilt with my Ladies armes waying twelve ounces and a half, an other guilt Casting bottle waying six ounces three quarters, an other guilt Casting bottle waying foure ounces & a quarter, a little bottle white waying foure ounces, a pepper boxe guilt waying too ounces three quarters, an other pepper boxe guilt waying foure ounces, an other pepper boxe with a spoone white waying too ounces, too Cupps of assaye guilt waying thirteene ounces & a quarter, an other Cup of assaye guilt waying eight ounces, too other Cups of assaye guilt waying thirtene ounces, a spitting Cup guilt waying eight ounces, a square Chafing dishe white and wrought waying fyftie fyve ounces and a half, an other Chafing dishe white waying twentie eight ounces, a Chafing dishe with a perfuming pan white waying thirtie three ounces, too long guilt Candlestickes waying threescore and too ounces, six Candlestickes wrought with stages and talbotes white waying twoo hundreth fortie ounces, six Candlestickes like gallies white waying Fourscore and too ounces, too wyer Candlestickes waying fyftene ounces, fowre white Candlestickes waying one hundredth seaven ounces and a half, An other white Candlestick waying eleven ounces. An other white Candlestick waying twentie ounces three quarters, an other white Candlestick waying thirtene ounces, too other white Candlestickes waying twentie and foure ounces, a little white Candlestick for waxe lightes waying three ounces, Fyve payre of white suffers waying twelve ounces and a half, a Chamber pott white waying nyntene ounces, a Lie pott with a glass and a place for

a Combe waying twentie ounces and a half, a Standishe white with dust
boxe & boxe to set pens in waying fortie too ounces, a Cristall trymmed
with silver and guilt & some pearle waying twentie too ounces and a half,
a grater white waying too ounces, a George guilt waying eleven ounces,
seaven tops for bottles white waying eleven ounces, a boxe for metredate
guilt waying fyve ounces & half a quarter, a boxe for metredate white
waying an ounce three quarters. A glass trymmed with silver and guilt
with a Cover and the Armes of England set in golde on the top, not wayed,
an oystridge egg, trymmed with silver and guilt with a Cover not wayed, a
Currall Rock, Eight stone Juges trymmed with silver and guilt not wayed,
a tosting forke of wood trymmed with silver.

Lynnen in the said newe building as followeth viz: in one Trunck, a peece
of fyne newe damask for table clothes of too yardes & a quarter brode,
and seventene yardes three quarters long, an other peece of fine newe
damask for table clothes of three yardes brode and nyne yardes and a half
long. An other peece of fyne newe damask for towells of twentie too
yardes long, an other peece of fyne new damask for towells of thirtie nyne
yardes long, an other peece of fine newe damask for towells of thirtie nyne
yardes long, an other pece of fyne newe damask for napkins twelve yardes
long, an other peece of fine newe damask for towells thirtie eight yards
long, a peece of fyne newe diaper for table clothes a yard & a half
brode and thirtie and one yardes long, an other peece of fine newe diaper
for a towell fyve yardes and a half long, an other peece of newe diaper for
towells too yardes & a half long, an other peece of diaper for napkins
rowde with blewe, fortie and one yardes long, a sheet to pack that stuff in.
In an other trunk bounde with Iron, a peece of newe damask for towells
nyne yardes three quarters long, an other peece of newe damask for
towells thirtie eight yardes three quarters long, an other peece of newe
damask for a towell thirtene yardes long, an other peece of newe damask
for table clothes too yardes and a quarter brode and thirtene yardes & a
half long, an other peece of newe damask for a table cloth too yardes and
a quarter brode, & three yardes three quarters long, an other peece of
newe damaske for table clothes, too yardes and more brode, and twelve
yardes long, a peece of newe diaper for table clothes too yardes and more
brode and thirtie yardes long, an other peece of diaper for a table cloth too
yardes and a quarter brode and sixe yardes long, an other peece of diaper
for towells thirtie eight yardes & a half long, an other peece of newe
diaper for towells thirtie eight yardes & a half long, an other peece of newe
diaper for towells thirtie eight yardes long, an other peece of diaper for
towells twentie one yardes & a half long, an other peece of newe diaper
for towells twentie sixe yardes long, an other peece of diaper for towells
twentie one yardes & a half long, an other peece of newe diaper for

towells twentie sixe yardes long, an other peece of diaper for towells thirtie fyve yardes three quarters long, an other peece of newe diaper for towells fortie yardes long, an other peece of newe damask for towells twentie yardes long, an other peece of newe damask for table clothes twentie yardes long, an other peece of newe diaper for a table cloth too yardes and more brode and too yardes and three quarters long, an other peece of newe diaper for a table cloth too yardes & more brode and too yardes three quarters long, an other peece of newe diaper for table clothes too yardes & more brode and Fourtene yardes long, an old diaper Cubberd cloth to Cover the stufe. In an other trunck a diaper table cloth too yardes brode, and sixe yardes & a half long, an other diaper table cloth too yardes brode and sixe yardes three quarters long, an other diaper table cloth, too yardes brode and six yardes and a quarter long, an other diaper table cloth nere too yardes brode and fyve yardes long, an other diaper table cloth nere too yardes brode and sixe yardes three quarters long, a table cloth of damask, too yardes and a quarter brode and six yardes long, an other damask table cloth too yardes and a quarter brode and seaven yardes and a quarter long, an other fayre long damask table cloth nere three yardes brode and eight yardes three quarters long, an other damask table cloth too yardes brode and eight yardes long, an other damask table cloth too yardes and a quarter brode and seaven yardes long, an other damask table cloth too yardes brode and seaven yardes long, an other damask table cloth too yardes and more brode and seaven yardes long, a diaper table cloth too yardes brode and sixe yardes and a half long, a diaper table cloth a yarde and a quarter brode and sixe yardes long, a damask towell seven yardes and more long, an other damask towell eight yardes & a half long, an other damask towell eight yardes long, an other damask towell eight yardes & a half long, an other damask towell eight yardes long, an other damask towell seaven yardes long, an other damask towell sixe yardes long, an other damask towell fyve yardes three quarters long, an other damask towell sixe yardes long, an other damask towell fyve yardes long, an other damask towell three yardes three quarters long, an other damask towell three yardes & a half long, seaventene other damask towells of too yardes long a peece, a diaper towell fyve yardes long, an other diaper towell sixe yardes three quarters long, a Cubberd Cloth of damask a yard & a half brode and too yardes long, sixe Cubberd Clothes of damask too yardes and a quarter long a peece, too other damask Clothes three yardes long, sixtene square clothes of diaper a yard and a half brode and too yardes long a peece, too square clothes of diaper, a yard & a half long and a yarde & a quarter brode a peece, sixe dozen and tenn diaper napkins, sixe dozen and eleven damask napkins, a long table cloth of lynnen, too yardes brode and sixe yardes long, a Cubberd cloth of damask to Cover the same lynnen. In an other trunck three table clothes of damask seven yardes long a peece, too table clothes of damask seven yardes and a half long a peece, too table clothes of damask, sixe yardes long a peece, one table cloth of damask fyve yardes three quarters long, a diaper table cloth of fyve yardes long, too other diaper table clothes of sixe yardes long a peece, too other diaper table Clothes seven yardes long a peece, an other diaper table cloth sixe yardes three quarters long, three damask towells eight yardes and a quarter long a peece, a damask towell sixe yardes & a half long, a damask towell nyne yardes long, a damask towell eight yardes & a half long, a damask towell fyve yardes & a half long, a damask towell sixe yardes long, a damask towell seven yardes and a quarter long, a damask towell sixe yardes and a quarter long, a damask towell foure yardes & more long, a square cloth of damask, too yardes and a quarter long, a diaper towell seven yardes long, a diaper table cloth, three yardes & a half long, a square cloth of diaper too yardes & a half long, a square cloth of diaper too yardes long, a table cloth of lynnen fowre yardes long, an other table cloth of lynnen sixe yardes and a half long, an other table cloth of lynnen sixe yardes & a half long, too other table clothes of lynnen sixe yardes & a half long a peece, a Cubberd Cloth of lynnen too yardes & a quarter long, a table cloth of lynnen foure yardes long, too Cubberd clothes of lynnen too yardes long a peece, a towell of lynnen cloth foure yardes long, a midling Sheet to Cover the same lynnen. In an other trunck a payre of verie fine Camebrick sheetes, a payre of fyne holland sheetes more, seven payre of fyne holland sheetes more, eight payre and a sheete more of holland sheetes not so fine, three playne Cambrick pilloweberes, tenn holland pilloweberes, a sweet bagg of Chaungeable taffetie, three Course sheetes in the bottom, a Cubberd cloth on the top, a Coverpane imbrodered with gilde and fayre wrought, an other Coverpane wrought with golde and silver and Coulored silkes, a fayre quition cloth wrought with golde and silver and red and grene silk, a Cubberd Cloth or quition cloth wrought with oring tawnie and red silk, an other Cubberd cloth wrought with golde and silver and watchet silk & edged with golde and silver, an other Cubberd Cloth all white worke and fringed with silver, an other Cubberd cloth, a napkin and a towell wrought with black silk. A Cubberd Cloth trymmed with golde bone lace and eglantynes of silver, too payre of sheetes wrought with Coulored silk, the one payre edged with golde lace, the other with Coulored silk, a payre of lardge pilloweberes wrought all over with black and red silk, an other payre of pilloweberes wrought all over with gold and red and grene silk, a payre of pilloweberes wrought with Carnation, grene, and yellowe silk, a payre of pilloweberes wrought with net worke and lawne, a payre of pillowberes wrought with red silk, a payre of pilloweberes wrought with red, blewe and grene spotes, a pillowbere wrought with golde and silke of divers Coulers, a payre of pilloweberes trymmed with a great golde lace, sixe pilloweberes trymmed with golde and silk lace, a little payre of pilloweberes not made up wrought all over with black silk. In an other trunck seven payre of good fine holland sheetes, fyve payre of holland sheetes, sixtene payre of lynnen sheetes, a table cloth of damask fyve yardes three quarters long, an other damask table cloth seven yardes and a quarter long, an other damask table cloth six yardes long, a Damask towell sixe yardes long, too damask towells fyve yardes long a peece, too diaper table clothes of sixe yardes and a quarter long a peece, too square fine diaper clothes, too fine diaper clothes three yardes brode and sixe yardes and a quarter long a peece, an other diaper cloth too yardes brode and sixe yardes long, a damask towell six yardes long, a damask towell too yardes long, thirtene damask napkins, too dozen and eight diaper napkins, sixtene pillow beres of holland, too diaper towells more, a lynnen towell.

Notes (by room number)

8 This chamber and the Room at the Wardrobe Door (13) could not both be by the Wardrobe (12), unless the clerks entered 12 and 13 in the wrong place.

21 The elaborate bed in this room was shaped like a ship.

23 This room was hung with five tapestries depicting the story of Tobit and his son, Tobias.

24 Although the clerks only describe the two tapestries as 'with personages', the name suggests that they were from a set illustrating the biblical story of Jacob.

35 A Closet within 34. These two rooms were as yet full of unpacked trunks and other goods. If Bess still had a personal maid in addition to her gentlewomen, she was not yet provided with a bed.

37 Bess's grand-daughter, Lady Arbella Stuart, was the child of Elizabeth Cavendish and Charles Stuart, 5th Earl of Lennox, the younger brother of Mary Queen of Scots' second husband, Henry Stuart, Lord Darnley. Through her father, Arbella had a claim to the English throne.

43 The Prodigal Chamber was hung with tapestries illustrating the Story of the Prodigal Son. Bess, who seems to have been attached to this parable, perhaps still hoped for the reform of her 'bad son Henry'.

46 This ground floor room was at the south end of the arcaded tarras or walk along the east front of the house.

47 The provision of a nursery suggests that Bess was expecting her son, William Cavendish, to bring his children to stay with her. He and his first wife, Anne Keighly, had had four: three boys and a girl. The two eldest, Gilbert and William, were in their early teens by 1601, but James, the youngest boy, and the girl, Frances, were young enough to need the nursery and to use the 'too Chares for Children' in their grandmother's withdrawing chamber.

63 Prepared food was set out in the Surveying Place ready to be transported in a ceremonial procession, under the direction of the surveyor or usher, to the Hall or other dining area. On formal occasions at Hardwick, it was carried the full width and height of the house to the High Great Chamber. There was an Usher's Chamber, convenient to the Hall, in the Old Hall (O.H.43).

Plate No location is given but, if this hugely valuable collection was not in the inner chambers to William Cavendish's Chamber (45), as suggested above, it is likely to have been in one of the two inner rooms (49 or 53) off the Pantry (52).

Linen This also represented a substantial capital investment. The eight trunks in which it was packed are likely to have been among those listed in the Maid's Chamber (34) and elsewhere in the immediate area of the Countess's Bed-chamber.

Plans of the New Hall

The numbers on the plans below follow the order of the 1601 inventory, which starts with one of the turrets on the roof (1) and ends with the Porter's Lodge (65). There are some problems, due partly to quirks on the part of the inventory clerks and partly to later alterations to the building.

The grandest rooms were at the top of the house and they included a set of fine guest rooms (4–6) in a then smaller area of what is now the attic floor. The Wardrobe (12) was in the same area but, while concentrating on the fine rooms, the clerks apparently forgot to list its contents until they were amongst the State Rooms on the floor below. Their route through the network of rooms at the south end of the first floor and at the north end of the ground floor is hard to follow, especially as both areas have been altered. One alteration that is clear is the flooring over of the central well in the floor of the Upper Chapel (26), from which the family had been able to look down onto the Lower Chapel on the ground floor (27).

The empty turrets on the roof are not listed, nor are two rooms which open off William Cavendish's room on the ground floor (45). One of these was eventually fitted-out as strong room and, if this was already done, then the plate, which is listed separately at the end of the inventory, was probably stored there.

The plans show all partition walls in their present positions except on the second and third floors, where alternative layouts have been tentatively suggested to accommodate the relocation of the Wardrobe and its adjacent rooms (7, 8, 11, 12, 13, 15). Work on the identification of the rooms is not fully complete and not all numbers have been allocated, notably in the area of the kitchens.

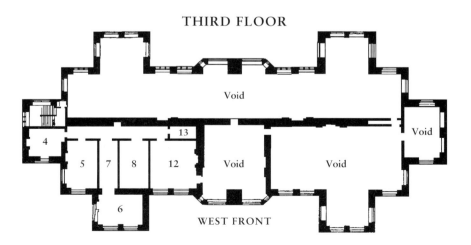

THIRD FLOOR

OF HOUSHOLD STUFF

SECOND FLOOR

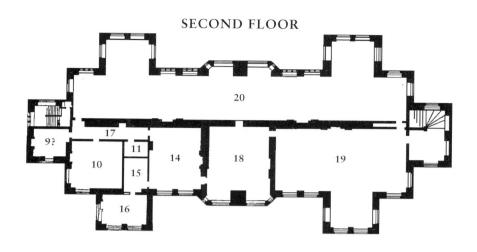

FIRST FLOOR

GROUND FLOOR

Glossary

Bill
long-handled weapon with concave blade carried by watchmen

Binges/bynges
bins

Bonelace
so called from the bone bobbins used in its making

Boulting byng
bin to hold flour or meal, also a sifting bin

Brandreth/brandyron
dialect word for a gridiron

Bridges
from Bruges. Usually 'Bridges sattin', a half silk much used for costume and upholstery

Caffa/Caffoy
a furnishing fabric of wool or wool and silk, with patterns imitating those of silk velvets

Carsey/Kersey
named after Kersey in Suffolk but, by the late 16th century, a widely-made coarse, twill-weave woollen cloth

Chamber
in most instances this term denotes the equivalent of a modern bed-sitting room, although it was also applied to grand rooms, such as the High Great Chamber. Bess and other important individuals had their own withdrawing chambers and bed-chambers

Ciphers
monograms

Closet
these small rooms, either within or adjacent to a chamber, were variously used to house a close-stool, provide storage space for clothes or accommodation for a servant

Coverpane
a linen cover, sometimes embroidered, used in formal dining to cover a place setting

Cuningree
a managed rabbit warren

Currall/carrill/carrell
listed with other mixed fabrics of silk, worsted and linen in the Norwich Drapers' Book of 1570

Darnix
from Doornick, the Flemish name for Tournai. An upholstery fabric of varying quality, usually made of linen and wool but sometimes incorporating silk and metal threads. It was used for wall and bed hangings and was decorated with relatively large patterns

Firkin
a small cask for liquid and such goods as fish; equal to a quarter of a barrel

Fledges
bed or floor covers made of a coarse woollen cloth called fledge. There were 'whoole clothes of fledge to make fledges of, peeces iij' recorded at Sheffield Castle in 1582

Forrest work
verdure tapestry

Fretts
a strapwork pattern

Fustian
cloth with a linen warp and cotton weft; sometimes including worsted wool. Also a blanket made from it

Kitte/kytt
circular vessel of hooped staves, with handles and sometimes a lid, for carrying milk and other commodities

Kymnell
dialect word for a tub, especially for salting meat or butter

Landyron/andiron
firedogs

Lie pot
for lie, an alkali solution concocted of urine and used for bleaching hair (hence the comb)

Lights
candles or tapers

Lystes
detached selvedges or strips of fabric. These were joined to make cushions and other items

Metredate
mithredate, a composition of many ingredients in the form of an electuary, regarded as a universal antidote or preservative against poison and infectious disease

Mockadoe
from the French, *moucade*. A woollen velvet, plain or patterned, the pattern either woven on the loom or stamped on with a heated metal plate

Murry
mulberry or morello coloured

Pallet
originally a straw mattress, which could be rolled up during the day. Most of those in the New Hall at Hardwick contained a mattress and other bedding, so they may have had a box-like frame, although they were not so elaborate as the 'too bedstedes to turne up like Chestes' on the staircase landing (N.H.40)

Panes
broad bands of contrasting colours; rectangular panels framed by another material

Pantes
from the French, *pentes*. The bases or lower valances of a bed

Parchment lace
a form of passementerie made with very narrow strips of parchment wrapped round with silk or metal threads and linked by thin silk or linen thread. Perhaps already made as a bobbin lace, as it was in the seventeenth century

Peniston
a woollen cloth, probably from Penistone in south Yorkshire

Pillowberes
pillowcases of linen

Plommier
plumber

Plummerie
plumber's workshop

Posnete
small metal pot with a handle and three feet, used for boiling. Cf. posset pot

Pullies (pair of)
uncertain, but protective knee armour was known as pulley pieces. The Hardwick pair was lined with black taffeta and was in the Countess's bed-chamber with her comb and mirror; it may have served to protect her knees, with which she was having trouble

Purl
coiled, spring-like metal thread (made of wire) with either a round or angular profile; used in short lengths or as raised loops or spots and couched down with a thread run through the centre of the coil

Rowde
a striped or ribbed effect

Saye
a light-weight, twill-woven woollen cloth resembling serge

Scarlet cloth
the most expensive form of woollen cloth; usually, but not always, dyed scarlet

Sestern
cistern, or sester (vessel for holding liquids or a dry measure for wheat); here probably a wine cooler

Sivine
raspberry

Slips
gardener's term for a cutting, used to describe detached needlework or cut-fabric sprigs

Spanish blanket
woollen blanket from Catalonia

Sparver
a bed-canopy suspended from the ceiling

Standard
a large chest or trunk

Strike
bundle of loose flax or hemp

Stythie
anvil

Tarras
a terrace or walk, usually arcaded. In the 16th century the term was one of several used in place of the Italian *loggia* and Smythson used it to describe the balustraded walk on top of the hall screen at Hardwick (N.H.30).

Tills
compartments or drawers within a chest or cupboard

Tissue
in sixteenth-century England this denoted an exceptionally elaborate fabric incorporating areas of raised looped pile of metal thread

Travice
a 'traverse' or partition, sometimes of wood but more often a curtain, to pull across a room as a divider or draught excluder

Turkie work
knotted pile fabric made in England (the industry later centred on Norwich). The inventory clerks carefully distinguished it from the 'Turkey carpets' imported from Asia Minor

Twist
a thick thread usually of silk and metal threads plied together, used extensively on furnishings decorated with embroidery and needlework

Valure
woollen velvet

Voyder
a vessel (in this case of copper) into which dirty dishes, utensils or fragments of food were placed in clearing a table

Wardrobe
a room used for the storage of spare furniture, textile furnishings and clothes

Washcoloured
probably pale blue, but uncertain how it differed from watchet. 'Wash', in its meaning of stale urine, was used as a mordant with indigo

Watchet
light blue, sometimes with a greenish tinge

Worte
a fusion of malt or other grain for beer

Bibliography

Beard, Geoffrey, *Upholsterers & Interior Furnishing in England 1530–1840*, Yale University Press, New Haven & London, (1997).

Digby, George W., *Elizabethan Embroidery*, Faber & Faber, London, (1963).

Durant, David N., *Bess of Hardwick*, Weidenfeld & Nicolson, London, (1977), revised paperback, Peter Owen, London, (1999).

Girouard, Mark, 'Elizabethan Chatsworth', *Country Life*, CLIV, (22 November 1973), pp. 1668–72.

Girouard, Mark, *Guide to Hardwick Hall*, The National Trust, (1972 & 1989).

Girouard, Mark, *Robert Smythson & The Elizabethan Country House,* Yale University Press, New Haven & London, (1983).

Levey, Santina M., *An Elizabethan Inheritance. The Hardwick Hall Textiles*, The National Trust, (1998).

Levey, Santina M., 'What the Selection Made by Survival Reveals', an analysis of the surviving stitched textiles at Hardwick Hall in Mary M. Brooks (ed), *Textiles Revealed. Object lessons in historic textile and costume research*, Archetype Publications, London, (2000).

Levey, Santina M., *Catalogue of the Sixteenth-Century Stitched Textiles at Hardwick Hall*, The National Trust, forthcoming.

Montgomery, Florence, *Textiles in America, 1650–1870*, W. W. Norton & Co., New York & London, (1984).

Thornton, P.K., 'Tapisseries de bergame.' *Pantheon, Internationale Zeitschrift für Kunst*, 18, (1960), 85–91.

Thornton, P.K., *Seventeenth-Century Interior Decoration in England, France & Holland*, Yale University Press, New Haven & London, (1978, paperback 1983).

Thornton, P.K., *The Italian Renaissance Interior 1400–1600*, Weidenfeld & Nicolson, London, (1991).

Worsley, Lucy, *Hardwick Old Hall*, English Heritage, (1998).